THE CHRISTIAN
ORTHODOX FAITH

THE CHRISTIAN ORTHODOX FAITH
BY ARCHIM. EPIPHANIOS K. HADJIYIANGOU
Tel.: +30) 697 968 9890.
email: epifanioshad@gmail.com

Translated by
Bishop PANTELEIMON Lampadarios,
Metropolitan of Antinoes

Edited by Holy Monastery of St. Augustine, Florina, Greece

1st Edition 2017
2nd Edition 2021

Title of the original Greek book:
Η ΟΡΘΟΔΟΞΗ ΠΙΣΤΗ ΜΑΣ

© KYPRIS X. & Co
   1 Avlonos & L. Katsoni str., 143 43 New Chalkidona, Athens-Greece
   tel. +30 210 8542020, fax: +30 210 8542071
   e-mail: skypris@otenet.gr, www.skypris.gr

ISBN: 978-618-5233-12-9

Publishing Production - Central stock: KYPRIS X. & Co.

ARCHIM. EPIPHANIOS K. HADJIYIANGOU

THE CHRISTIAN ORTHODOX FAITH

Translated by
Bishop PANTELEIMON Lampadarios,
Metropolitan of Antinoes

Greetings from His Eminence
Metropolitan Theocletos
of Florina, Prespa and Eordaia

Before His Ascension, our Lord Jesus Christ said to His holy apostles, *"Go therefore and make disciples of all the nations, baptizing them in the name of the Father and of the Son and of the Holy Spirit, teaching them to observe all things that I have commanded you; and lo, I am with you always even to the end of the age. Amen."* (Matt. 28:19-20).

From the time the holy apostles received this commandment, they went out to the entire world preaching the word of our Lord. The phrase: *"Their line has gone out through all the earth, and their words to the end of the world"* (Ps. 18/(19):4) foretells the event of the spreading of the Holy Gospel.

Thus all the earth became a school of Christ. Men who followed the new Faith became disciples. The holy apostles taught and the Christians became disciples in Christ's school, listening to the words of the Holy Gospel. With this new Faith, and not religion, the Kingdom of Christ was established on earth.

Generally, the essence of the new Faith was composed of what was believed and practiced. Faith, as something intangible and theoretical, was proven through the complete change of the way of life of all those who were previously idol-worshippers; men and women of all ages, who lived the rest of their life in Christ. The Life of Christ became their life. Everyone received strength to continue their struggle from the continuous reminder of the word of God, either written or oral.

St. Luke the evangelist and apostle, wrote in his Gospel to the noble Theophilos, *"that you may know the certainty of those things in which you were instructed"* (Lk. 1:4). St. Peter wrote, *"though you know them, and are established in the present truth... I will be careful to ensure that you always have a reminder of these things"* (2Pt. 1:12-15).

Preaching, the word of God and catechising were the vital responsibilities of the Church of Christ, and not inventions of the heretics who appeared much later. Thus, the shepherds safe-guarded their flock from the spiritual wolves who tried to infest the fold of Christ.

Beloved,

I wrote all the above desiring to emphasize the just praise of the local Church to the writer of this blessed work. The writer, Archim. Epiphanios, is dear to us for many years now. Cypriot by birth, from youth he toiled to teach the children of the Ecclesiastical School of Florina and the parishioners of the Cathedral of St. Panteleimon of the city of Florina. His book is the fruit of many years of work. It was written after much research of patristic sources as well as the Church's dogmatic texts. It methodically presents with complete order, clarity and accuracy, the doctrines of the Church, analyzing the Holy Creed, which contains briefly everything necessary that a Christian is required to know, believe and practice.

Granting our Episcopal blessings for the publishing of this important work of our beloved Fr. Epiphanios, we fervently pray for the spiritual benefit of all those who study it. We are proud of him for completing such an important work and we urge him to bring forth more such works for the glory of our Lord and the benefit of souls. Amen.

In Florina the 18th October 2015, St. Luke the Evangelist.
With heartfelt prayers to the Lord

THE METROPOLITAN

+Metropolitan THEOCLETOS
of Florina, Prespa and Eordaia

*This book is dedicated to the memory
of my respected mother **Eleni Hadjiyiangou,**
who by her word and example,
taught me faith in God.*

Archim. Epiphanios K. Hadjiyiangou

INDEX

PROLOGUE TO THE ENGLISH EDITION

This book first circulated about a year ago in the Greek language with the title "Η ΟΡΘΟΔΟΖΗ ΠΙΣΤΗ ΜΑΣ", so that the Greek people could learn about their Orthodox Christian Faith. Many people who live overseas pleaded with us to translate the book into English so that the newer generations, who don't know Greek very well, can read it. So we decided to translate it. Consequently this book is now addressed not only to Greeks, but to everyone, whether Orthodox or not, who would like to learn about Orthodoxy.

I would like to warmly thank His Grace Panteleimon, Metropolitan of Antinoes, for his delighted acceptance to translate the book from Greek into English, and the effort he exerted to do this.

I would also like to thank the English speaking sisters at the Holy Monastery of St. Augustine in Florina, for editing the translation.

Florina, November 2016

Archim. Epiphanios Hadjiyiangou

PROLOGUE TO THE GREEK EDITION

It is commonly acknowledged that our Orthodox faithful, in their majority, lack catechism (i.e. instruction in our Faith). Although concerning science, technology, computers etc., most people, especially the youth of today, are well informed and knowledgeable; concerning faith they are still deeply ignorant, even of the basic truths.

This is the main cause of the spreading of heresies in our country, which unfortunately grow, luring those who have no catechism and those who are weak members of the flock of Christ, our Orthodox Church.

There are different reasons for this ignorance. Family, school, the government, and others, are responsible. The Church has a great responsibility, and especially the clergy who, besides our liturgical and administrative duties, have a basic duty to *"preach the gospel"* (Mk. 16:15), i.e. to teach and to instruct.

Who does not admire and also does not reproach himself because of the missionary work of the great teacher of the Greek Nation, St. Cosmas Aitolos, who *alone* managed to change the course of Greek history and prevented complete Islamization, a danger which the Greek Nation faced. He traveled all of Greece by foot, and with his simple but warm words achieved the spiritual regeneration of our enslaved country. It is not an exaggeration to say that, in this case, *"the people who sat in darkness saw a great light and upon those who sat in the region and shadow of death, Light has dawned"* (Matt. 4:16). So, if today we had such teachers of the divine word, *"full of divine zeal"* (St. John Chrysostom), our country would be in a much different condition. Consequently, it is necessary for a **re-evangelization** of and within the Orthodox Christian world.

This book was written with the purpose of presenting briefly and simply our Orthodox Christian Faith. It contains a brief description of 100 sermons on the Holy Creed, which, with the blessings of His Eminence Metropolitan Theocletos of Florina, Prespa and Eordaia, I delivered as evening homilies in the holy Cathedral of St. Panteleimon, Florina, between 2007-2013.

I hope that this humble effort will contribute to the acquaintance of our people with our Orthodox Faith, which will protect them from the various heresies, –which as Lernaean Hydras threaten them– and which will free them from the errors and superstitions which are rooted within. *"Know the truth and the truth will set you free"* (Jn. 8:32).

I feel the need to express my gratitude to His Eminence Metropolitan Theocletos of Florina, Prespa and Eordaia for His support in this effort, as well as for the honor of addressing with pastoral greetings, the introduction of this book.

I also thank the *protoshingel (chancellor)* of the Metropolis, Archim. Nikiforos Manadis for his various recommendations.

I especially express my gratitude to my spiritual brother, Archim. Lavrentios Gratsias, for his essential contribution to this publication.

In Florina, October, 2015

Archim. Epiphanios K. Hadjiyiangou

1. INTRODUCTION

1.1. ORTHODOX CHRISTIAN CATECHISM

*"The Christian way of life depends on two things: **correct doctrines** and **good deeds.** And neither the doctrines without the good deeds are pleasing to God, nor the good deeds which are performed without correct doctrines are acceptable to God"* (St. Cyril of Jerusalem).

Consequently, every Christian must know these two things very well: correct doctrine (= correct faith) and good deeds (= correct way of life). Both are equally necessary for our salvation.

Orthodox Christian Catechism aims to teach these topics; **orthodoxy** (=correct faith) and **orthopraxia** (=correct deeds). In this book we shall learn briefly about our Orthodox Christian Faith. As our basis, we shall have the **Holy Creed** for guidance.

The Holy Fathers of the Church

1.2. THE SOURCES OF CATECHISM

Orthodox Christian Catechism (religious instruction) is based upon Holy Scripture and Sacred Tradition.

A. **Holy Scripture**

Holy Scripture is the w r i t t e n   w o r d of God to man. It is the sacred Book written by men enlightened by the Holy Spirit. It contains the Old and New Testaments.

The **Old Testament** contains the work of God before the coming of Christ into the world and has forty-nine Books. Of these, some are h i s t o r i c a l, some are d i d a c t i c (instructive) and others are p r o p h e t i c.

The **New Testament** contains the life and work of Christ, the life of the first Church and the Epistles of the Apostles, and contains twenty-seven Books.

Holy Scripture is G o d - i n s p i r e d. It was written, as we have mentioned, by men who were enlightened by the Holy Spirit. Consequently, everything that it contains is true.

B. **Sacred Tradition**

Sacred Tradition is the u n w r i t t e n w o r d o f G o d, i.e. the oral teachings of Christ and His Apostles. Sacred Tradition includes the decisions of the Oecumenical and Local Synods, the Holy Creed, as well as other practices of the Church, such as making the sign of the Holy Cross, celebration of the Divine Liturgy etc.

Authentic Sacred Tradition was preserved only by the Orthodox Church, for the Protestants renounce Sacred Tradition entirely, whereas the Roman Catholics added many new doctrines which are alien to Holy Scripture and Sacred Tradition (Filioque [= the proceeding of the Holy Spirit from the Father and the Son], the infallibility of the Pope, purgatory, etc.). We will refer to this in chapter 17.4.

1.3. THE HOLY CREED

Meaning

The **Holy Creed** is a written text, which contains briefly all the basic truths (doctrines) of our faith. It contains everything that an Orthodox Christian believes.

The Holy Creed was composed by the holy Fathers of the 1st and 2nd Oecumenical Synods, in the year 325 AD and 381 AD and has **twelve articles**.

The Holy Creed

1. *I believe in one God, the Father Almighty, Maker of heaven and earth, and of all things visible and invisible.*

2. *And in one Lord Jesus Christ, the Son of God, the Only-begotten, who was begotten of the Father before all ages. Light of light, true God of true God; begotten, not made, of the same essence as the Father, through whom all things were made.*

3. *Who for us men and for our salvation came down from heaven and was incarnate of the Holy Spirit and the Virgin Mary and became man.*

4. *And was crucified for us under Pontius Pilot, and suffered and was buried.*

5. *And rose on the third day according to the Scriptures.*

6. *And ascended into heaven and sitteth at the right hand of the Father.*

7. *And He shall come again with glory to judge both the living and the dead, Whose Kingdom shall have no end.*

8. *And in the Holy Spirit, the Lord, the giver of Life who proceedeth from the Father, Who with the Father and the Son is together worshipped and glorified, Who spoke through the prophets.*

9. *In One, Holy, Catholic and Apostolic Church.*

10. *I acknowledge one baptism for the remission of sins.*

11. *I look for the Resurrection of the dead.*

12. *And the life of the age to come. Amen.*

2. GOD

1. *"I believe in one God"*

2.1. THE EXISTENCE OF GOD

Testimonies about the existence of God

The Holy Creed begins with the phrase: *"I believe in one God."* The primary and basic truth of our faith is that God exists (see Heb. 11:6). How can we be assured of this? No-one can see God for *"He is spirit"* (Jn. 4:24), but He reveals Himself to man through His works.

The first way which God reveals Himself to man is through the **physical world**. This immense and wondrous universe which we see around us, with its billions of stars and galaxies, with its or-der and harmony, with its amazing laws with which it is governed; the Earth with its hundreds of thousands of living species; each and everyone one of them —especially man— is a miracle concerning its construction and function. All of these bear testimony to the existence of one All-wise and Almighty God Who created them (see Wis. 13:5; Rom. 1:20).

And as a painting was painted by someone, or a watch was made by someone, likewise someone created the physical world. St. Paul teaches that: *"Every house is built by someone, but He Who built all things is God"* (Heb. 3:4).

History also bears witness to the existence of God. Generally, in all the nations, from ancient times until this day, people believe in a Higher Power. Everyone accepts that there is a God. This belief was expressed by the ancient Greek historian Plutarch with one of his memorable texts:

"Wandering around the world, one can find cities without walls, without script, without rulers, without houses, without properties, with no need of currency, not knowing about theaters and gymnasiums; but a city without altars and gods, which does not pray ... no-one ever saw, nor will ever exist" (Ethics VI, 2, 173, To Koloti [in Greek]).

Finally, faith in God is found engraved deep in the **soul** of all men. It is asserted by the conscience, the inner voice which informs us what is good and what is evil, and as an invisible judge, judges our deeds. It is revealed by the desires of our heart, which is not satisfied with material goods and pleasures, but with the presence of God.

2.2. THE ESSENCE AND ENERGIES OF GOD

What is God? – Essence and Energies of God

But what is God? No-one knows. It is beyond man's capabilities to fully know God. Although we know that *there is* a God, we do not know *what is* God. But why should we wonder? There are so many things around us that we do not understand. What is matter? What is light? What is electricity? No-one knows. *"If it is impossible to count the stars of heaven and the drops of rain, how can you want to understand God? Look at the sun, if you can. How can you demand to see God?"* (St. Cyril of Jerusalem).

The holy Fathers of the Church made a distinction between the **essence** of God and His **energies**. The essence of God differs from the energies of God. The essence of God is unknown and inconceivable. On the other hand, the energies of God can be known and conceivable to man.

2.3. THE DIVINE ATTRIBUTES

The energies of God are also called attributes and they are divided into natural, logical and ethical. Following, we will examine a few of them, the most well-known.

A. **Natural attributes**

a. God is **Omnipresent**. He exists everywhere. There is no place in the universe where God is not present. When we say God "dwells" in the heavens, or in the temple, we mean that His presence is expressed more there.

b. Another natural attribute of God is that He is **Omnipotent**. He can do everything. Nothing is impossible for God.

c. God is **eternal.** All things have a beginning and an end, but *God has no beginning nor end* (see Rev. 1:4).

God is also **immutable** and **unalterable**. He does not perish, nor does He change. On the contrary, the world perishes and changes.

B. **Logical attributes**

a. God is **Omniscient**. As the Creator of the universe, He knows everything and to a perfect degree. He knows the past, the present and the future. He even knows the most secret thoughts of men (see Ps. 138/(139):2,5,16).

God knows in advance the events which will take place in the future, but without causing them. God knows, but never predestines. Consequently, the foreknowledge of God does not annul man's free will.

b. God is **All-wise.** God's wisdom is revealed within the natural world, as we mentioned above. Even more admirable is the plan of Divine *Economy (Dispensation)*. In other words, the way in which God wanted to save man through Christ's sacrificial Crucifixion on the Cross, as we will examine later on.

C. **Moral attributes**

a. God is perfectly **holy.** He has no association with evil and sin. He is All-good and sinless.

b. God is **All-true.** He has no association with falsehood and hypocrisy. Christ Himself said: *"I am the truth"* (Jn. 14:6). God is also **faithful**; in other words He is steadfast. He keeps His word and fulfills all His promises, both blessings and threats.

c. God is absolutely **righteous** (Ps. 10/(11):7). He desires that moral order rule in the world. Consequently, He ascribes justice to everyone, according to their deeds.

Why does He allow evil and injustice to prevail in the world? We will examine the answer to this question in another chapter.

d. The most important and most characteristic attribute of God is **love**. *"God is love"* (I Jn. 4:16). He created man out of His love. For man's sake God created the beautiful world in which we live. Out of love, He provides for all His creatures, even for the most insignificant (Matt. 10:29). God's love is especially revealed, in that for our sake he sent His Only-begotten Son into the world, Who was crucified for our sins (see Jn. 3:16).

2.4. THE TRIUNE GOD

The doctrine of the Holy Trinity

We have stressed that the primary truth of our faith is that God exists. As the Holy Bible reveals to us, God is **One** and not many (see Dt. 32:39, Jn. 17:3). The second basic truth is the doctrine of the **Holy Trinity**. In other words, that God is one according to His essence (nature), but three persons: **Father, Son** and **Holy Spirit**. God is, as we say, *Triune*. One God exists in three persons (hypostases).

The Holy Trinity depicted in the form of three angels which Abraham gave hospitality to

The three persons or *hypostases* of the Holy Trinity are *homoousia* (of the same essence). They have the same essence and all attributes in common. No person of the Holy Trinity is inferior to the other. The Father is perfect God, the Son is perfect God and the Holy Spirit is perfect God. They also have common will and energy. In other words, in all the energies of God, e.g. in the creation of the universe, all three persons participate.

The principal source of the deity is the Father. The other two persons originate from the Father. Specifically, the Son is "begotten" of the Father and the Holy Spirit "proceeds" from the Father.

We confess the Holy Trinity in our prayers and worship. *"Glory to the Father and to the Son and to the Holy Spirit...,"* *"In the name of the Father and of the Son and of the Holy Spirit...,"* etc. The Holy Trinity is symbolized with the three fingers as we sign ourselves with the sign of the holy cross.

The Holy Trinity in Holy Scripture

When Christ sent the apostles to preach the Gospel, He said: *"Go and make disciples of all nations, baptizing them in the **name** of the **Father** and of the **Son** and of the **Holy Spirit**"* (Matt. 28:19). We notice that, although Christ uses the single form: *"in the name,"* after that He refers not to one, but three names: *"of the Father and of the Son and of the Holy Spirit."* This reveals that God is one in essence but three in persons (see 2Cor. 13:14 [or verse 13 in Greek]).

Besides the above, we have the revelation of the Holy Trinity during the Baptism of Christ in the Jordan River. The **Son** was baptized, the **Father** gave witness, and the **Holy Spirit** in the form of a dove certified this.

3. THE CREATION OF THE WORLD

"Maker of heaven and earth, and of all things visible and invisible."

3.1. CREATION IN GENERAL

God is the Creator of the world

God is the Creator of the whole world; both visible and invisible. The natural world (the universe), as well as the spiritual world (the angels), are God's creation. This great truth is revealed to us by the first verse of Holy Scripture: *"In the beginning God made the heavens and the earth"* (Gen. 1:1).

God created the universe o u t o f n o t h i n g, without pre-existing matter (see II Macc. 7:28). He created it o n l y by H i s w o r d, with the command *"Let there be..."* (see Ps. 148:5, 32/(33):6).

The creation of the world according to Holy Scripture

According to Holy Scripture, the world was made in **six days**. We do not know exactly what six days means; it is suggested to be a long period of time. On the first day God created the light. On the second day, He created the firmament (the atmosphere) which separated the waters from above the firmament (the clouds) and below the firmament (rivers, oceans etc.). On the third day, the separation between land and sea took place, and the earth sprouted and bore fruit. On the fourth day, the sun, the moon and the stars appeared. On the fifth day, God created the fish and the birds. Finally, on the sixth day, God created the terrestrial animals and man.

As we can see, God created the world gradually, beginning from the more simple and imperfect and proceeding to the more complex and perfect. Finally, He created man, the most perfect of all His creatures.

The meaning of Creation.

What is the purpose of Creation? Why did God make the world? He made it o u t o f l o v e. He who loves, desires to share his goods with others. Thus God, Who is Love, wanted other creatures to partake of His blessedness. The world is an overflow of God's love.

3.2. THE ANGELS

The angels and their work

According to the teachings of Holy Scripture, God's first creations were the angels. He created them before the creation of the visible world (see Job 38:7, Col. 1:16).

The angels are immaterial and immortal beings. They do not have needs according to nature, they are not subject to the laws of nature and they are much more powerful than man (see Ps. 102/(103):20, II Kings 19:35, Gen. 19:11).

The angels are also rational beings and have free will as do men; that's why they have the possibility to remain and progress in goodness, but also to choose evil. One can see this with the fall of Lucifer, as we will mention later on.

There are **nine hosts** of angels: Angels, Archangels, Rulers, Authorities, Powers, Dominions/Principalities, Thrones, Cherubim and Seraphim. We know the names of three Archangels: Michael, Gabriel and Raphael.

The work of the angels is twofold. Firstly, they ceaselessly worship God (see the vision of the prophet Isaiah Ch. 6). Secondly, they conduct work concerning man's salvation (see Heb. 1:14), either conveying God's messages to man, or protecting him from natural or spiritual dangers.

Every believer, from the day of his baptism until the end of his earthly life, has a **guardian angel**.

The angels in Holy Scripture.

Throughout Holy Scripture, from the first Book, —Genesis—until the last —the Revelation of John— there are many cases where angels appeared: Jacob's Ladder, the Annunciation of the Theotokos, the appearance of angels to the shepherds at Bethlehem, appearing to the Myrrh-bearing women, in the revelation to St. John; and will appear at the Second Coming of the Lord, etc.

3.3. THE DEMONS

The demons and their fall

The demons are spirits, as are the angels, but evil. However God didn't create them like that. In the beginning they were good angels, unaware of evil. Unfortunately, they made bad use of their free will. Their leader, Lucifer, out of pride wanted to become like God (see Is. 14:13-14). As soon as he had this thought, he fell *"as lightning"* from heaven and became the Devil or Satan. When he fell, he misled many angels with him. (see Lk. 10:18, Rev. 12:4).

All these angels fell into the darkness of Hades, and from angels of light became evil *"angels of the abyss,"* the dark demons (Jude 1:6, 2Pt. 2:4, Rev. 9:1-11).

The work of the demons and deliverance from them

The demons, after their fall, wanted to drive man to evil, therefore Satan, through false promises, misled the first-created man to sin. Thus evil and death entered the world. But Christ, through His death on the Cross and His Resurrection, abolished death and the authority of Satan.

After the redeeming work of Christ, the power of the demons was significantly, but not entirely, limited. They are able, with God's concession, to tempt man, but they cannot force anyone to perform evil. With God's grace a Christian can be victorious over the devil.

4. MAN

The creation of Man

Once God had created everything, visible and invisible, finally, on the sixth day, He created man. He created him in a special way. God took earth and formed his body. Next God breathed in his face the *"breath of life"* (Gen. 1:26 & 2:7). These two acts show that man is made of two elements: body and soul.

God also created woman in a specific way. He put Adam in a deep sleep and took one of his ribs, from which He formed Eve (see Gen. 2:21-22). This reveals that woman is of the same substance and nature of man. She is not an inferior creature, as many ancient philosophers have stated.

The fact that God took one of Adam's ribs reveals the e q u a l i t y between woman and man. The woman originated from the side of the heart, which reveals the love which the husband should have towards his wife. Finally, God made only one woman for man; consequently ruling out polygamy.

Man's body

Although man's body is made out of the dust of the earth, it has great value. Firstly, its stature reveals its divine origin. Of all the animals, only man walks upright, in order to look towards heaven, his eternal homeland.

The body is the t e m p l e o f G o d (1Cor. 6:19) and not the soul's prison, as was believed by many philosophers. Also, it is sanctified through the Holy Sacraments and especially by

Holy Communion. And finally, one day the body will be res-urrected and will enjoy eternal life together with the soul. Consequently, we must respect and take care of our bodies. It is forbidden to harm ourselves in any way, and of course suicide is completely forbidden. Above all, we must preserve our bodies pure from carnal sins (see 1Cor. 6:18; 1Th. 4:4).

Man's soul

The superiority of man in relation to the other animals is not owing so much to his body, but to his soul. But is there a soul? Yes there is. This is testified by:

a. Holy Scripture. Christ said: *"Do not fear those who kill the body but cannot kill the soul"* (Matt. 10:28, see also Matt. 26:41; Acts 7:59; 1Cor. 6:20).

b. The faith of all mankind. From ancient times until this day, every religion of all nations, accepts that there is a soul which lives even after death.

c. The manifestations of the soul. Man is not satis-fied only with material goods, as the animals are. He thirsts to know the truth. He seeks God and wants to be united with Him. The animals don't think, and for centuries live in the same way. Man thinks, judges, fantasizes, creates and progresses. Although he is a weak creature, he subdues even the most powerful ani-mals; he overcomes the powers of nature.

But, **what is the soul?** It is *"simple substance, bodiless, invis-ible, logical..., and uses as its instrument of expression the body"* (St. John Damascene). The soul has free will. It can choose freely between good and bad. Through the soul, man communicates with and worships God.

The soul is created and united with the body from the mo-ment of conception. That is why abortion is murder. The soul is in all of the body and is separated from the body at the time of death.

The *"in the image"*

According to Holy Scripture, man was created *"in the image"* and *"likeness"* of God (Gen. 1:26).

"In the image" signifies that man is a living image of God. He has by nature, divine attributes. This is a great honor for man. These divine attributes which God gave man, are mainly the nous (intellect), so as to think and judge; free will, with which he has the ability to choose between good and evil; and supremacy over the natural environment.

Since man is the image of God, we must honor and respect each person. Every action which insults man, insults God Himself, Who created him.

The *"in the likeness"*

Man's purpose is to use the gifts which were given to him by God in order to become *"in the likeness"* of God, that is, to become similar to Him: just, good, merciful, and in a word, to become holy. That's why Holy Scripture teaches us: *"Be holy, for I am Holy"* (1Pt. 1:16. see also Lev. 20:7). In other words, man's purpose is to progress from being *"in the image"* of God, to reaching the *"likeness"* of God. The *"in the image"* is an exclusive gift of God. The *"in the likeness"* is the result of God's grace in co-operation with man's efforts.

The *"in the image"* therefore, refers to man's nature, whereas the *"in the likeness"* refers to man's destiny.

5. DIVINE PROVIDENCE

5.1. GOD AS PRESERVER AND GOVERNER OF THE WORLD

The meaning of Divine Providence

God is also "Pantocrator" (Almighty). He is called this because He governs everything. Once He created the world, He did not then abandon it. He continues to oversee the world and takes an interest in it. This interest and continuing care of God for the world is called **Divine Providence**. Without Divine Providence the universe would have remained ungoverned and would have been destroyed.

Divine Providence extends throughout all of creation, from the largest to the smallest things (see Ps. 103/(104); 144/(145):14-16). If God provides for the least of all things, how much more does He provide for man! Let us recall the Lord's poignant words: *"Look at the birds of the air, for they neither sow nor reap nor gather into barns; yet your heavenly Father feeds them. Are you not of more value than they?"* (Matt. 6:26-30).

Every man, if he examines his past, will see that many times God has benefitted him and protected him from danger. And even in national and global history we see God providing for and guiding the course of the world. Also, there are moments when people abandon us, but God never abandons us.

Manifestations of Divine Providence

Divine Providence is expressed in two ways: God m a i n t a i n s the world, in order to preserve it throughout the ages; and God also g o v e r n s the world – in other words he guides it to the purpose for which He created it.

However, Divine Providence is revealed mainly in what God did for man's salvation. God did not abandon His creation after Adam sinned. He sent His Only-begotten Son, our Lord Jesus Christ, into the world, to save us (Jn. 3:16).

Although God preserves and governs the world, He does not abolish man's free will. He respects our decisions and actions; He tolerates our mistakes and continuously gives us opportunities for repentance. Without pressuring us, He implants within us good thoughts and takes measures to guide us to Him, despite our personal errors or our errors as a nation.

Prayer and miracles

If there wasn't Divine Providence, then prayer would have no meaning. We pray because we believe that God provides for the world and especially for man, who He follows in all his steps in life. If our prayer is addressed with faith, then God intervenes, putting aside the natural laws, and saves us. This extraordinary intervention of God is what we call a miracle. Our life is full of miracles.

5.2. WHY DOES EVIL EXIST IN THE WORLD?

We raise the question however: since God provides for and takes care of the world, why does evil exist in the world? Why should n a t u r a l e v i l exist; e.g. earthquakes, floods, droughts, pain, illnesses, etc.? Why should m o r a l e v i l exist; e.g. injustice, poverty, crime, wars, etc.?

The answer to this question is not easy. Generally one can say the following: Firstly, for God, the basic subject is not how long or in which way we shall live this life; our purpose is to inherit His Eternal Kingdom. Secondly, for God, the greatest evil is sin, because all the other evils torment man temporarily, whereas sin will cause him to suffer eternally.

St. Basil the Great, speaking about natural evil, teaches us that God allows it mainly to limit sin; e.g. an earthquake or other natural catastrophes have as their result to limit sin to a certain degree. Secondly, He allows it to bring the rest of mankind to its senses. Sometimes God allows natural evil to occur to test our faith; in other cases, to recognize our sinfulness and so lead us to repentance. There are many cases where a serious illness brought man closer to God (see Is. 26:16. Prov. 23:14).

Concerning moral evil (injustice, crimes, wars, etc.), God is not the cause of it, but man himself. God allows it because He respects our freedom. If God prevented man from doing evil, man would stop being free, he would cease to be man; he would become a robot.

6. PARADISE AND THE FALL OF FIRST MAN

6.1. PARADISE

When God created the *protoplastous* (first man), **Adam** and **Eve,** He placed them in a beautiful Garden which He prepared for them on earth —**Paradise**— which was *"eastward,"* (Gen. 2:8) and charged them to cultivate and protect it (see Gen. 2:15).

Adam and Eve *"were both naked... and were not ashamed"* (Gen. 2:25), *"for they were vested with divine glory"* (St. John Chrysostom).

Path to God

In Paradise man lived in unlimited joy and blessedness. He was in perfect harmony with himself, with God and with the natural environment.

Man's condition in Paradise was not static. Every day, he would progress and he would proceed, to reach his highest purpose, the *"in the likeness,"* and perfect union with God. This would have been achieved with God's help but also with his personal efforts.

For this reason, God gave one commandment to Adam and Eve, which they had to keep in order to prove their faith and love for Him.

The two trees of Paradise

In Paradise two separate trees are mentioned: the *"tree of life"* and the *"tree of knowledge of good and evil."* The *"tree of knowledge of good and evil"* was one of the many trees of Paradise. It received this name, because whosoever would eat of its fruit would experience what is good and what is evil. The other tree was the *"tree of life."* The fruit of this tree was a unique gift: to transmit eternal life. He who would partake of its fruit would become immortal.

6.2. THE ANCESTRAL (ORIGINAL) SIN

Unfortunately the blessed life of Paradise did not last long. Adam and Eve were deceived by the devil and disobeyed God's commandment and so sinned. This became the reason for them to be exiled from Paradise, to live with labor and pain, and finally to face death. Let us examine this tragic event, the Ancestral sin, as it is called.

The commandment, the tempter and the fall

The commandment which God gave to Adam and Eve instructed that, *"from every tree of the garden you may freely eat; but from the tree of the knowledge of good and evil you shall not eat, for in the day that you eat the fruit of it you shall surely die"* (Gen. 2:16-17).

The **temptation** and the **fall** of mankind followed. *"Now the serpent was more cunning than any beast of the field which the Lord God had made. And he said to the woman, 'Has God indeed said, 'You shall not eat from every tree of the garden?'*

And the woman said to the serpent, 'We may eat the fruit of the trees of the garden; but of the fruit of the tree which is in the midst of the garden, God has said, You shall not eat it, nor shall you touch it, lest you die.'

And the serpent said to the woman, 'You will not surely die. For God knows that in the day you eat it your eyes will be opened, and you will be like God, knowing good and evil.'

So when the woman saw that the tree was good for food, that it was pleasant to the eyes, and a tree desirable to make one wise, she took its fruit and ate. She also gave it to her husband with her, and he ate.

Then the eyes of both of them were opened, and they knew that they were naked; and they sewed fig leaves together and made themselves coverings." (Gen. 3:1-7).

As we can see, he who caused man to sin was the devil, the hater of good. His means were crafty. He spoke with seeming interest for man. But behind that hid his hatred for man. He told lies, slandering God as being jealous. Finally, he deceived man, because he promised him that he would become God.

The devil chose to deceive the woman first, because she was easier to convince. He found her alone, because that way it was easier to deceive her. As soon as Eve sinned, she wanted to mislead her husband into sin. Of course Adam is also responsible; he should have resisted Eve's proposition and should have remained faithful to His Creator's commandment. Unfortunately, he also desired to become God.

In the end, the sin was performed, which was disobedience and unfaithfulness to God, Who created them and granted them so many blessings. But the first man showed obedience and trust to an unknown creature, and in essence wanted to satisfy his own egotism. Man wanted to become God, but alone, without God.

6.3. THE CONSEQUENCES OF ANCESTRAL SIN

The "judgment" of the First Man

Instantly, as soon as Adam and Eve sinned, they realized that they were naked, for they had lost the grace of God and their innocence. Simultaneously, they felt guilt and fear, thus they hid themselves when they heard God's voice calling them.

God asked them why they ate the forbidden fruit. Adam answered: *"The woman whom you gave to be with me, she gave me the fruit of the tree, and I ate."* Eve answered: *"The serpent deceived me and I ate"* (Gen. 3:12-13). Both avoided their responsibilities. But no-one forced them to sin. The violation of the commandment was purely their free choice.

The "first good news"

God said to the serpent: *"I will put enmity between you and the woman, and between your seed and her Seed; He shall bruise your head and you shall bruise his heel"* (Gen. 3:15).

These words are very important. They prophesy a future conflict, by which man's salvation will be achieved.

The exile of Adam and Eve

God refers to an enmity which will be created one day between Satan and a woman. This woman is *Panagia* (the Virgin Mary). The *"seed"* (descendent) of the woman, is Christ (Gal. 3:16). *"He shall bruise your head and you shall bruise his heel"* (Gen. 3:15). These words forewarned the complete destruction of Satan by Christ. Satan would only be able to *"bruise Christ's heel,"* in other words to harm Him with a small injury. This is the prophesy of the death of the Lord on the Cross, which would end on the third day with His Resurrection.

As we can see, immediately after the fall of Adam and Eve, God announced the good news of the coming of the Savior, Who would crush Satan and save the world. Thus, this promise, which is the first good news to man, is called the "proto-evangelion."

This first good news survived throughout history and became legend to all the nations; that's why the coming of the Savior was the desire and hope of the entire world.

Man's punishment

After the fall, God said to the woman: *"I will greatly multiply your pain and your groaning, and in pain you shall bring forth children. Your recourse will be to your husband and he shall rule over you"* (Gen. 3:16). The woman sinned first, thus she received the first punishment. She was punished as a mother to bear children with pain. She was punished as a wife to submit to her husband, because she misled him to sin.

And to Adam, God said*: "Because you have heeded the voice of your wife…, cursed is the ground for your sake. In toil you shall eat from it all the days of your life. Both thorns and thistles it shall bring forth for you, and you shall eat the herb of the field"* (Gen. 3:17-18). As we can see, after sin, nature rebelled and became hostile towards man. Plants and animals became dangerous and/or lethal. The ruler became a slave. Consequently we have the "natural evil" of which we have spoken.

God continues, saying: *"In the sweat of your face you shall eat [your] bread"* (Gen. 3:19). From this we can see that the bread that is produced with hard work and sweat is blessed. Whatever is the fruit of theft or easy profit, e.g. with lottery or gambling, is not blessed. Then God announced that one day man will surely die: *"…till you return to the ground. For out of it you were taken. For dust you are and to dust you shall return"* (Gen. 3:18-19). This is the most serious of all the punishments mentioned previously.

Along with mankind, the entire natural world (the animals, plants and all God's creatures) would follow the path leading to decay and death (see Rom. 8:19-22).

The exile of the First Man from Paradise

Following this sin, Adam and Eve were exiled from Paradise. God *"sent him out of the garden of Eden to till the ground from which he was taken"* (Gen. 3:23).

What a tragic moment! The king of all Creation is dethroned. He is found suddenly outside of Paradise and is exiled to *"the land of the shadow of death"* (Is. 9:2). Naked and deprived of every good, he is condemned to live with hard work, tears and pain, until he is led to the frightful end – death. Behold the results of sin.

The spiritual consequences of the Fall

1. **Spiritual death.** As soon as Adam sinned, he immediately died spiritually; his spirit was separated from God; consequently he felt naked, guilty, etc. His biological death (the separation of the soul from its body) came much later.

2. **The distorting of the *"in the image."*** With sin, the divine image which man had, was disfigured. Specifically: a) Man's n o u s (the soul's eye), by which he saw and communicated with God, was darkened, and he turned to the worshipping of false gods. Man could no longer distinguish between good and evil. b) Man's h e a r t was corrupted. It lost the purity and innocence which it had in Paradise, and is now ruled by passions, evilness, filthy desires, etc. c) Man's w i l l was enslaved by evil. Although before the fall he was well disposed towards good, now he is enslaved to the inferior way of life: sin.

Despite all this, the *"in the image"* was not completely lost. Within man remained some powers and abilities of good, which keep the soul from complete enslavement to evil. Between these two forces a harsh inner warfare takes place (see Rom. 7:14-24).

Transmission of the Ancestral sin to the human race

The Ancestral sin was transmitted to the entire human race as an inherited illness, because in the person of Adam, all mankind sinned (Rom. 5:12). And as a tree with a rotten root produces rotten fruit, it is the same with Adam: as the root of mankind, he was condemned to impart his sinful nature, decay and death, to all his physical descendants. Nobody is exempt from this universal law, except for our Lord Jesus Christ.

6.4. THE GRADUAL CORRUPTION OF THE HUMAN RACE

Idolatry

When men multiplied and scattered over the face of all the earth, they ceased to worship the true God and began to worship the natural forces: the sun, stars, mountains, animals, etc. They even worshipped lifeless statues (idols), which they made themselves; they worshipped and venerated them as gods! To these false deities men offered unlimited animal sacrifices,  even humans. Idolatry, according to St. Gregory the Theologian, is the extreme degeneration of logical man.

Moral corruption

Because of idolatry, God abandoned man, resulting in him committing the most shameful and unspeakable deeds, which lower him to the level of animals (Ps. 48/(49):12). The peak of this moral corruption was *"vile passions"* (Rom. 1:26), the committing of abnormal sins. Sin spread as a contagious illness to the entire earth (Ps. 13/(14):1-3).

Social corruption

With the above came social corruption. Men became cruel and unsociable, like the beasts. They lost all sense of what it meant to be human. They believed that their s l a v e s were *res* (objects). They bought and sold them, and they could do whatever they wanted to them, even kill them. W o m e n had no rights. Many even doubted if women were people. Besides this, there was also polygamy, which was humiliating for women. C h i l d r e n were also considered worthless and not protected. Many were offered as sacrifices to the false gods, being burnt alive.

Cruelty, injustice, and exploitation had reached the point of no return. Pain, hopelessness and desperation ruled everywhere. Society had become a form of hell. Many people committed suicide. Satobrian, a French writer of the 18th century, characteristically said: *"If Christ had come a little bit later, He would have found only the carcass of society."*

This briefly, was the religious, moral and social situation in which mankind was led after the Ancestral Sin.

7. MAN'S REDEMPTION

7.1. THE WORK OF DIVINE ECONOMY (DISPENSATION)

No-one was able to save man from the above situation. This is when the infinite wisdom and the inconceivable love of God was revealed. God found the way to cure the situation. God sent His Son into the world to save us (see Is. 63:9). This work of God to save man from sin is called **"Divine Economy"** or **"the work of redemption."** God had thought of this before all ages, because He knew that Adam and Eve would fall even before He created them.

The Nativity of Christ

What exactly took place? The Son and Word of God, the second person of the Holy Trinity, became man. He became perfect man and lived amongst us. Through His teachings, He revealed to us the true God. By His crucifixion and death, He became victorious over Satan and abolished sin. With His Resurrection, He abolished death. By His Ascension, He raised man to Heaven.

7.2. THE PREPARATION FOR SALVATION

Let us examine now: how did God prepare mankind to receive the Savior and Redeemer? The first ray of hope was given by God in Paradise with the **"first good news" ("the proto-evangelion")** which we mentioned previously.

Later, God chose one nation, the **Israelites**, who became the chosen people of God. He had chosen them to become the "ark" of the true faith, with the ultimate plan that from them would come Christ, the Savior of the world. God ensured this nation was kept from the idolatry and moral corruption in which all the other nations were enslaved. Thus God frequently sent them prophets, He gave them the Old Testament Law and He taught them using both blessings and punishments, in order to keep them close to Him.

Also, God did not abandon the other nations, the **"gentiles."** God gave them the innate law of conscience (Rom. 2: 15). He also preserved within them two feelings: guilt for sin and the hope of salvation.

Other means which God used to prepare the gentiles were the following: a) The philosophers. They were inspired individuals who taught higher moral and religious ideas. b) The Jews of the diaspora who were scattered all over the world. Through them many gentiles discerned the true God. c) The global political situation. When Christ came there was one universal empire, the Roman; and one international language, the Greek; which assisted with communication and dealings amongst the nations. d) The Greek civilization and its philosophy, which Alexander the Great spread, which raised the spiritual level of the people. That's why many consider Alexander the Great as the forerunner of Christ.

The prophesies, an indisputable miracle

The prophets were messengers of God and spoke about the coming of the Messiah (Christ) to the Israelites. They lived hundreds of years before Christ. Some prophesied about Christ's birth, others about His life and His work, others about His Passion, His Resurrection, etc.

Prophesies are a unique phenomenon in history. In no other religion or for any other person do we have prophesies. According to historians, the prophesies are considered the first and greatest miracle in universal history.

The hope of the whole world

The hope for the Savior was not found only in the nation of Israel. A Savior was expected by all the nations. What is wondrous is that the people in the West expected the Savior from the East, whereas the people in the East expected Him from the West, in such a way that the hopes of all pointed to Palestine!

We find expectations of the Savior not only in the Old Testament, but also in the writings of many other ancient civilizations. They speak about the appearance of a god who will become man to deliver people from their sufferings. The most prophesies, and the clearest, were in ancient Greece. Some of them exist in Aeschylus' tragedy "Prometheus bound," as well as the works of Plato: "Apology of Socrates" and "The Republic" (Socratic dialogue).

In all these marvellous ways, God prepared the world to accept the Savior and Redeemer, and He constantly renewed this hope. From generation to generation one voice of hope was transmitted: *"He is coming!"*

And finally, He came. The Heavens opened and an angel of the Lord announced the good news to the shepherds of Bethlehem, the message which had been awaited throughout the centuries: *"For there is born to you this day in the city of David* [Bethlehem] *a Savior"* (Lk. 2:10-11).

8. OUR LORD JESUS CHRIST
2. *"And in one Lord Jesus Christ..."*

8.1. THE PERSON OF CHRIST

Introduction to the 2ⁿᵈ article of the Holy Creed

In the 2ⁿᵈ article of the Holy Creed the divinity of our Lord Jesus Christ is emphasized. Christ's divinity is the basis on which the Christian Faith is founded, and the basis of Christ's redemptive work. If Christ was not perfect God but a simple  creation, He could not have saved the world. Consequently, our Faith would be futile.

Historical testimonies of Christ

Some say that Christ never existed. But this is not true. The fact that Christ really existed as a historical person is witnessed by many Jewish and Roman historians. Besides, if Christ had never existed, His birth would not have divided the world's history into Before Christ (BC) and after Christ (AD).

The official and authentic sources and testimonies about Christ are the Books of the New Testament and especially the four Gospels. They were written by the eyewitnesses (apostles Matthew and John) or by those who heard them (Mark, Luke).

The authors of the Gospels, and all the apostles, did not hesitate to sacrifice their lives upholding the truth of these testimonies, a fact which certifies that they were absolutely sure of everything that they testified to, and consequently their testimonies are truthful.

The unique person of Christ

The person of Jesus Christ is unique in the world's history. In His person the two natures, divine and human, were united. Christ is God and man; p e r f e c t G o d and p e r f e c t m a n. As God, He was begotten of the Father before all ages. As man, He was born of the Virgin Mary over 2000 years ago.

In Holy Scripture we see Him appear with both natures. In some situations He acts as God (performs miracles, forgives sins, knows the thoughts of men); in other situations He acts as man (hungers, thirsts, becomes tired, sleeps, suffers, dies).

8.2. THE DIVINE NATURE OF CHRIST

Let us examine one by one the phrases of the 2ⁿᵈ article of the Holy Creed.

"In one Lord." Christ is *"Lord,"* in other words He is the Ruler of Creation. And indeed He is the one and only Lord. After His Resurrection He said to His disciples: *"All authority has been given to me in heaven and on earth"* (Matt. 28:18; see also 1Cor. 8:6-7; Rom. 14:9; Rev. 19:11-16 etc.).

"Jesus." The word *"Jesus"* is Hebrew and means "God saves," or "Savior." It is the name given to the Lord at His circumcision, according to the Law of God (Matt. 1:21).

Christ is truly "Jesus," absolutely Savior in all its meaning, for He saved the world from sin (Matt. 1:21; see also Acts 4:12).

"Christ." The word *"Christ"* is a Greek word which means "he who has been anointed." In the Old Testament, *"Christ the Lord"* was someone who, by God's commandment, was anointed with special oil to become a prophet, high priest, or king. Jesus is *"Christ the Lord"* in the absolute and full meaning. He was anointed by God with the Holy Spirit. With this anointment He received the three great offices or ministries: the Prophetic, that

of High Priest and the Royal. (Is. 61:1; Lk. 4:18; see also Ps. 44/ (45):7). In Hebrew the word *"Christ"* means "Messiah" (Jn. 4:25).

"the Son of God." Christ is not merely a great saint or prophet. He is the Son of God. At Christ's Baptism, as well as during the Transfiguration, God the Father called Him *"my beloved Son"* (Matt. 3:17; 17:5 see also Jn. 20:31, and also Matt. 26:63-64).

Certainly, all men are sons of God and especially the faithful. But Christ is by n a t u r e S o n of God. We are all a d o p t e d s o n s, *"sons by grace"* (see Jn. 1:12; Gal. 4:4-5).

"The Only-begotten." Our Lord Jesus Christ is the Only-begotten Son of God, according to the Gospel: *"God so loved the world that He gave His Only-begotten Son..."* (Jn. 3:16; see also 1:18; 1:14).

"Who was begotten of the Father before all ages." The Only-begotten Son of God was born of the Father before all ages. The Father speaks to the Son saying: *"Before I made the stars, before all time, I have begotten you"* (Ps. 109/(110):3 see also Prov. 8:23-25).

St. Cyril of Jerusalem teaches us, saying: *"When you hear that God begets, do not imagine a bodily birth... "God is Spirit" and the birth is spiritual."*

"Light of Light." Christ is *"Light of Light."* In other words, He is Light which originates from the Light, the Father. Christ Himself says that He is *"the Light of the world"* (Jn. 8:12; see also 1:9; Heb. 1:3).

"True God of true God." Christ is true God, Who came from the true God, the Father (I Jn. 5:20).

The divinity of Jesus Christ, this great doctrine of our faith, is attested to in many verses of the New Testament as well as in the Old Testament, such as: *"...and the Word was God"* (Jn. 1:1). St. Thomas confessed that Christ is his *"Lord and God"* (Jn. 20:28).

Because many heretics (for example the Jehovas' Witnesses) deny Christ's divinity, we quote a few verses from Holy Scripture:

Rom. 9:5; Col. 2:9; 1Ti. 3:16; Tts. 2:13; Ps. 44/(45):7 (see Heb. 1:8). Is. 9:6; Bar. 3:36-38; Is. 40:3; Is. 35:4-6.

"Begotten, not made." The Son was begotten of the Father; He was not made, as the material world was. That's why the article is supplemented by:

"of the same essence as the Father." As that which is born from man is man, likewise that which is born from God is God *homoousios*, in other words "of the same essence" with the Father Who begot Him.

"through Whom all things were made." Here we confess that the creation of all the world was made through the Son (Jn. 1:3; see Col. 1:16).

9. THE DIVINE INCARNATION

3. *"Who for us men and for our salvation came down from heaven, and was incarnate of the Holy Spirit and the Virgin Mary and became man."*

9.1. THE CONCEPTION AND INCARNATION OF THE DIVINE WORD

The Word of God becomes Flesh

St. John the Evangelist teaches: *"and the Word became flesh and dwelt among us"* (Jn. 1:14). In other words, the Son and Word of God, the second person of the Holy Trinity, became man and lived among us. This event is called the i n c a r n a t i o n of the Son and Word of God and consists of the fundamental truth of the Christian Faith. The whole deity descended to earth, but simultaneously remained wholly in heaven.

What was the reason that made God descend to Earth and become man? He came *"for us men and for our salvation."* He came to save mankind. He came to search for *"the lost sheep"* (see Lk. 15:3-6) and to bring it back to the heavenly fold, to Paradise.

The event of the Annunciation

When the time was proper, God sent the archangel Gabriel to the Virgin Mary and announced His great decision to her: *"You will conceive in your womb and bring forth a Son, and shall call his name Jesus; ... he will reign... forever, and of His Kingdom there will be no end"* (Lk. 1:30-33).

The Virgin, hearing these words, wondered: *"How can this be, since I do not know a man?"* And Gabriel said: *"The Holy Spirit will come upon*

The Annunciation of the Theotokos

you and the power of the Highest will overshadow you." Mary then said: *"'Behold the maidservant of the Lord! Let it be to me according to your word.' And the angel departed from her"* (Lk. 1:38).

After these words the Holy Spirit came to her, which cleansed her and released her from the Ancestral Sin. Then, the *"power of the Highest,"* the Son and Word of God, overshadowed her and created for Himself, from the pure blood of the Virgin Mary, a perfect human body with a logical soul (His human nature). In this body, the Son of God Himself entered and united with it (St. John Damascene).

Two natures, one person

As we can see, in the person of Christ, two natures are united: the divine and the human. Christ is perfect God and perfect man, **God-Man.** The two natures of Christ are united indivisibly and inseparably, without however, any confusion or one of them changing the other.

Although Christ has two natures, He does not have two persons, but one, that of the Son and Word of God, which He had before His incarnation. So Christ has t w o n a t u r e s (substances) but is o n e p e r s o n (one hypostasis).

The Divine Incarnation is a great and unfathomable mystery. God was manifested with human flesh! (1Ti. 3:16). How did this take place? Logically it is unexplainable. Only through faith can we begin to approach our understanding of it.

9.2. THE HUMAN NATURE OF CHRIST

Testimonies in Holy Scripture concerning Christ's human nature

In Holy Scripture there are many testimonies concerning the human nature of Christ. We see Christ being born, growing, eating, drinking, sleeping, being tired, sweating, suffering, dying, etc. All these show that He has a b o d y just like all men. On the other hand, we see Him progressing in knowledge, sympathizing with others, weeping, feeling holy wrath, etc. All these prove that He has a genuine s o u l with all its expressions. Consequently, He is perfect man, with a body and soul. Other verses in the Bible also certify to Christ's human nature, such as: 1Ti. 2:5; 3:16. 1Pt. 2:24, and many more.

The heresy of Monophysitism

As there are heretics who renounce the *divine* nature of Christ (Arius, the Jehovas Witnesses, and others), likewise there are heretics who renounce the *human* nature of Christ. The Monophysites accept only the divine nature, thus they are called **"monophysites" (mono=one phsyi=nature)**. Such mono-physites today are the Coptics of Egypt and the Armenians.

Christ is sinless

Christ is perfect man similar in everything to us but without sin. He is absolutely sinless (Heb. 4:15). *"...who committed no sin, nor was guile found in His mouth"* (Is. 53:9; see 1Pt. 2:22 and Jn. 8:46). Neither did He have the Ancestral Sin which all men inherit; because He was not born according to natural laws, by the union of man and woman; He was born *"of the Holy Spirit and the Virgin Mary."*

Christ is our *prototype* (archetype)

Christ as the perfect man is the perfect example in life which we are called to copy and imitate (1Pt. 2:21). With Christ as the archetype, man once again becomes man, in the full meaning of the word. When he is far from Christ, man becomes inhumane.

Also, since Christ is real and sinless, we should not doubt the truths which He revealed to us. We should be certain that eve-rything that He promised will be fulfilled (the end of the world, the second coming, Paradise, Hell, etc.).

Furthermore, since He is man as we are, He fully knows our human nature and can understand us and help us in every weak-ness or need (Heb. 2:18).

The three births of Christ

Christ is God and man. Consequently He has two births; He was born as God, and He was born as man.

As God, He is begotten of the Father *"before all ages."* As man, He was born of the Virgin Mary at a certain point in time (approx. 2,000 years ago). As God, He is begotten only from the Father, without a mother, while as man, He was born only from a mother, without a father.

Besides these two births, however, there is another third birth. It is the birth of Christ within the heart of every Christian, of which St. Paul speaks (see Gal. 4:19). The two births of Christ are great and admirable; but they have no essential meaning in our life if the third birth does not occur. And how will God be born? He will be born by our keeping of God's commandments, with ceaseless prayer and participation in Holy Communion.

9.3. THE ALL-HOLY THEOTOKOS
"and the Virgin Mary..."

Mary, the Ever-Virgin and Theotokos

The 3rd article of the Holy Creed refers to the Ever-Virgin Mary and Theotokos (Mother of God), the person who played the most important role in the work of man's salvation. Panagia became the "ladder" by which God came down to earth. She is the one who, amongst all women of all times was deemed worthy to become the mother of the Son of God. The Ever-Virgin is the most perfect and holiest creation of God which the world ever saw.

The Ever-virginity of the Theotokos

Another mystery which is related to the Divine Incarnation is that Christ was born from a virgin mother. The Virgin Mary was a virgin before childbirth, a virgin during childbirth, and remained a virgin after childbirth – in other words she is ever-virgin. Thus, two contradicting conditions are present in the person of the

Most Holy Theotokos: virginity and motherhood. She is simultaneously a mother and a virgin.

The ever-virginity of the Theotokos was prophesied in the Old Testament (see Is. 7:14) and is asserted in the New Testament (see Lk. 1:34. Matt. 1:18; 1:20 and 1:24-25).

The birth of Christ the Savior from a virgin mother is a great miracle. It is a mystery unexplainable by natural laws, which we must approach with faith and piety, without doubts, since nothing is impossible for God.

The place of the Ever-Virgin within the Orthodox Faith

The Orthodox Church follows the middle path in this situation also. The Church does not worship Mary as the Papists do, almost deifying the Mother of God; but neither does the Orthodox Church underestimate her as in Protestantism, where they consider her as merely a common woman.

The Orthodox Christian, without deifying the Theotokos, has her at the peak of all beings, higher and more holy than the angels and archangels: *"more honorable than the Cherubim and more glorious than the Seraphim"* (hymn to the Theotokos). She is the spiritual treasury of all virtues, that's why the entire Orthodox world honors her. Many glorious women were forgotten but the humble maiden of Nazareth remains alive in peoples' hearts throughout the ages and is glorified as no other person.

10. CHRIST AS TEACHER AND PROPHET

Christ heals man's *nous* (mind)

As we have mentioned, sin primarily wounded man's nous, that's why Christ began the work of redemption by healing the nous. The nous is healed and enlightened with the light of truth, with the word of God.

Christ's teachings

Once the Lord was baptized in the Jordan River, He chose twelve disciples and began his preaching, travelling throughout Palestine. For three years He taught the people, who thirsted to learn the truth. The people who heard His teachings were astonished. His teachings were nothing like that of the Scribes and Pharisees (Matt. 7:28-29).

Let us briefly examine the content of His teachings. Firstly, He revealed that God is Spirit, with love being the main characteristic. He spoke about the soul, about life after death, the Future Judgment, Paradise, Hell, etc.

Christ taught us that the first and most important commandment is to love God with all our heart. The second commandment is to love our neighbor as ourselves (Matt. 22:37-40). He also taught us that man does not find happiness in wealth, glory or material pleasures. Blessed are the humble, the meek, the just, the merciful, the pure in heart, those who have love in their heart (see Matt. 5:3-10).

Besides being a teacher, the Lord was a prophet. He foretold His Passion, His Resurrection, and the Second Coming. He prophesied the destruction of Jerusalem, the persecutions against the Christians, the final victory of the Church, etc.

The Lord confirmed His teachings with His miracles. Also, He Himself practiced what He taught, that's why His teachings had an impact on peoples' souls.

The eternal words which He spoke, were recorded by the holy evangelists and the Church preserved them unadulterated until this day. It is our duty to study and practice them in our daily life (see Ps. 1:2).

The results of the Christian Teaching

Other wise-men have also taught eloquently, but were unable to influence a person for the better. Only Christ's teaching has the power to transform souls, to change peoples' morals, and to comfort them. Millions of people who read the Gospel repented, believed and changed their way of life. This shows that Christ's teaching has divine origins.

Christ's teachings prevail regardless of the persecutions

The Christian teaching has endured and prevailed regardless of the many persecutions which it has been suffering for the past two thousand years. No other philosophy and no other religion has been persecuted as the Christian faith; and no other book has been warred against as much as the Holy Bible. Despite this, no one has been able to eradicate Christianity. This proves that Jesus Christ is not a simple man; He is also God.

11. THE WORK OF CHRIST AS HIGH-PRIEST

4. "And was crucified for us under Pontius Pilot,
and suffered and was buried."

11.1. THE SACRIFICE OF CHRIST AND ITS RESULTS

Christ's Sacrifice in general

Christ's teaching, however, was not enough to save man. Sin, the greatest obstacle between man and God, had to be overcome.

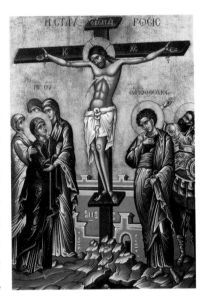

Sin was abolished completely with Christ's Sacrifice on the Cross. The blood which the God-Man shed at Golgotha washed away the sins of all men and reconciled man with God. St. John the Evangelist characteristically says: *"the blood of Jesus Christ his Son cleanses us from all sin"* (I Jn. 1:7).

The characteristics of Christ's Sacrifice

After Christ taught for three years, performed miracles and left us with a perfect example of holy life, He proceeded towards the Passion, to offer Himself as a sacrifice on the Cross.

Christ's Sacrifice was "r e d e e m i n g ." In other words, He was sacrificed for us to free us from our sins and to reconcile us with God. *"for if when we were enemies we were reconciled to God through the death of his Son, much more, having been reconciled, we shall be saved by his life"* (Rom. 5:10. see Is. 53:4-7).

The Lord's Sacrifice was also "r e p r e s e n t a t i v e ," for He sacrificed Himself to free *us*. He voluntarily took upon Himself the sins of all men as representative of the whole of mankind; *"that if one died for all, then all died"* (2Cor. 5:14).

Christ suffered v o l u n t a r i l y. He *wanted* to be crucified, without anyone compelling Him. Also, the Lord's Passion was the pinnacle of His l o v e towards man, as St. John teaches us, saying: *"for God so loved the world that he gave his Only-begotten Son, that whoever believes in him should not perish but have everlasting life"* (Jn. 3:16. see Rom. 5:8).

The result of Christ's Sacrifice

St. John Chrysostom teaches that with the sacrifice of Christ *"the tyranny of Satan fell, death was obliterated, sin was abolished, the curse ceased and Paradise was opened. Men and angels were united, the wall which separated us was torn down, and the God of peace reconciled the above and the below."*

Since Christ sacrificed Himself out of His love for us and gave us so many blessings and goods, we must feel infinitely grateful to Him. We should continuously thank Him in word and deed, and not disappoint Him with our sins. St. Paul teaches that all who were baptized, received the Holy Spirit and lived the Christian way of life; and if after that they were to sin again, they would be re-crucifying the Son of God (Heb. 6:6). So, every time that we sin, we crucify Christ again!

Christ's Sacrifice is relived during every Divine Liturgy

Christ was crucified once but it is valid for *"all eternity."* Christians throughout the ages re-live this during the Mystery of the Holy Eucharist. During the Divine Liturgy, the Holy Altar becomes the Golgotha on which the bloodless sacrifice of the Lord is offered.

11.2. THE DESCENT OF CHRIST INTO HADES

Christ's death

Once Christ said His last words on the Cross —the *"it is finished"*— *"He bowed His head and gave up His spirit"* (Jn. 19:30). With His death, His soul separated from His body, as occurs with all men. His body was placed in the tomb, whereas His soul descended into Hades.

But Christ was not merely man; He was also God. His human nature was inseparably united with His divine nature. Consequently, the divine nature of Christ continued to be united with His soul which went to Hades, but also with His body which remained in the tomb. The result of this union was that Christ's body did not decay, as occurs with the bodies of all men who die, but remained completely incorruptible (see Ps. 15/(16): 9-10).

The redeeming descent of Christ into Hades

When Holy Scripture speaks about *"Hades"* it implies the place where the souls went after death. It was a condition where sadness, pain and loneliness prevailed as a result of the absence of God. We do not know where Hades was.

The souls of all men, both sinners and the righteous, went to Hades. Christ had to preach the truth to them, as He did on earth. Before Christ, St. John the Forerunner had gone to Hades in order to prepare them.

So the great moment, which they awaited for centuries, arrived. Christ's soul, u n i t e d   w i t h   H i s   d i v i n i t y, descended into the dark kingdom of Hades. He descended to fight the great battle even there. And just as He was victorious over the devil on earth, likewise He also had to destroy the devil's main authority in Hades, and to free the souls who would believe in Him.

Hades could not have any authority whatsoever over Christ, because His soul was sinless, but also because it was united with the deity. St. Nicodemus the Athonite teaches us saying: *"If the soul of Christ was not united with the deity, then it would have been held by the bonds of Hades, just as the rest of the souls of the righteous who had died. But because it was united with the deity, not only did Christ put to death Hades by the 'lightning of His divinity,' not only was His soul not held in bondage, but all those souls who were held there, as in a prison, were freed and were raised with Him"* (Eortodromion).

We do not know what the content of Christ's teaching in Hades was. Neither do we know who and how many were saved. Whoever accepted His teachings and believed, was freed from the bonds of Hades and followed Christ to Paradise.

12. CHRIST'S RESURRECTION

5. *"And rose on the third day according to the Scriptures."*

12.1. CHRIST'S RESURRECTION AND ITS RESULTS

The meaning of the Lord's resurrection

Three days after Christ's death, He r o s e. That is, His soul returned to His body which was in the tomb and brought it back to life. Of course, other dead people had been resurrected before Christ (e.g. Lazarus) – the difference being that all of them died again later. But Christ does not die, He lives forever (Rom. 6:9).

The Resurrection of our Lord – pulling Adam and Eve out of Hades

Christ's Resurrection consists of the most important stage of the work of Divine *Economy (Dispensation)*. With His Resurrection, Christ c o n q u e r e d   d e a t h, that great evil which sin caused. Christ's Resurrection also proves that He is God, and that the Heavenly Father accepted His Sacrifice.

The resurrection of the dead

Christ's Resurrection is a world-saving event, for it also ensures *our* resurrection. In other words, the Lord did not raise only

Himself, but also resurrected the whole human race (see 1Cor. 15:21-22). Whoever believes in Christ and becomes a member of His Church and partakes of His Body and Blood, will be raised as Christ was risen. The God-inspired words of Holy Scripture assure us of this (see Rom. 6:3-8. Jn. 6:54).

Consequently, death is no longer a permanent condition but temporary. Death is *"a great sleep,"* as St. Cosmas Aitolos said. For this reason concerning the dead, we use the term *"sleeping"* and graveyards are called "cemeteries" which in Greek literally means "places of *sleeping."[kimitiria]*

The importance of Christ's Resurrection

The event of the Resurrection comprises the basis of our faith and the foundation of the Church. Thus the message of the Resurrection is the major theme of the Apostles' preaching (see 1Cor. 15:3-4). As the apostle Paul emphasizes, if Christ was not raised, then our Faith would be in vain (see 1Cor. 15:17). If Christ did not rise, then neither will the dead rise, and so the struggle which any Christian goes through would have no meaning.

Since, therefore, the Lord's Resurrection is the basis of the whole of Christianity, it is logical that it would subsequently be doubted and persecuted more than any other truth of our Faith. That's why we shall present a few testimonies concerning Christ's Resurrection, below.

12.2. TESTIMONIES CONCERNING CHRIST'S RESURRECTION

The Empty Tomb testifies to Christ's Resurrection

The Body of Christ was not found in the Tomb on that Sunday morning. What happened? Was it stolen by the disciples? That was impossible, for the disciples, out of their fear, had closed themselves in a house and didn't dare to go out (Jn. 20:19).

Perhaps it was stolen by the Jews? Then let them present Him, in order to prove the apostles wrong, who preached that

He rose from the dead. What then became of the Body of Christ? There is only one answer: He rose from the dead!

The eleven appearances of the risen Christ

After Christ's Resurrection He did not ascend immediately into Heaven; He remained on earth for forty days, so as to convince His disciples that He is truly risen (Acts 1:3). Eleven appearances are recorded in Holy Scripture: He appeared to Mary Magdalene, to Peter, to the disciples without and then with Thomas, to more than five hundred people... and finally to the apostle Paul.

The change which took place in the souls of the disciples

When Christ was captured, the disciples out of fear ran to hide. A little while later, however, we see an amazing change in their mentality. Those who previously had no courage, those timid hares, suddenly became lions, bold preachers of the Resurrection (see Acts 2:22-24,36; 4:10). And not only did they fearlessly preach the Resurrection, but because of this they endured persecutions and finally death. It is not possible for a man to willingly sacrifice himself for something that he knows isn't true.

The spreading of the Gospel

Another proof concerning the Resurrection is the spreading of the Gospel and the triumph of the Church. The spreading of Christianity by twelve simple fishermen who managed in a small period of time to change an entire world sunk in errors and immorality, is impossible to humanly achieve. It is an miracle which was achieved by the Risen Christ.

In addition, the apostles faced strong opposition from the Jews and also from the Roman Authority. It is estimated that there are millions of martyrs who shed their blood for their Faith. How many people fought against the Church? How many persecutions were proclaimed? How many tyrants, of both old and recent times, have not used every satanic method in order to destroy the fold of Christ? Where are all of these? They disappeared and were forgotten. What happened to the Church? It shines more than the sun. The twelve lambs of Christ managed to be victorious over the wolves. How did this happen? There is only one answer: *"Christ is risen!"*

12.3. PROPHESIES CONCERNING THE RESURRECTION

In the Holy Creed we confess: *"And rose on the third day according to the Scriptures,"* that is, according to the prophesies of the Old Testament.

The event of the Resurrection, as well as the entire work of Christ, has been prophesied in the Old Testament. A few of these prophesies are found in: Psalm 15/(16):8-10; 29/(30):4. Is. 63:11.

The most well-known prophecy prefiguring the resurrection of Christ is that of the prophet Jonah. Just as Jonah remained in the beast's belly for three days and afterwards he came out alive, likewise Christ remained in the tomb for three days and then was resurrected (Matt. 12:40).

13. THE ASCENSION OF THE LORD

6. "And ascended into heaven and sitteth at the right hand of the Father."

The historical event of the Ascension

Forty days after Christ's Resurrection, He took His disciples to the Mount of Olives. Once He told them His last words, He raised up His hands and blessed them (Lk. 24:50). *"Now it came to pass, while he blessed them, that he was parted from them and carried up into heaven"* (Lk. 24:51). At one point a cloud took Him and hid Him from their eyes forever (Acts 1:9); and as they watched, having their eyes turned towards heaven, two angels appeared

The Ascension of our Lord

in white clothing and said to them: *"Men of Galilee, why do you stand gazing up into heaven? This same Jesus, who was taken up from you into heaven, will so come in like manner as you saw him go into heaven"* (Acts 1:11).

With Christ's Ascension, He rose above the angels and archangels and *"sat down at the right hand of God"* the Father (Mk. 16:19). He sat on the throne of God, partaking as man, in the glory which He had as God.

The meaning of the Ascension

As we can see, there are two ladders in the redemptive work of Christ. The first is the ladder of His d e s c e n t down to earth and the second is the ladder of His a s c e n t, or rather, His return to Heaven. There is, however, one basic difference between His descent and ascent. Before He descended to earth, Christ was only with His Divine Nature, without a human body; but when He ascended into Heaven, He also had His human nature united with His Divinity. In other words, Christ descended as G o d and ascended as G o d - M a n .

The Ascension consists of the completion of the redemptive work of the Lord and the purpose of the Divine Incarnation, which was to take fallen man from the depths, where sin had lowered him, and raise him to God's throne.

The gifts of the Ascension
a. The sending of the Holy Spirit

The first —immense— gift which was offered by the Ascension of the Lord is the Holy Spirit, Who came to establish the Church and to continue Christ's work.

b. The securing of a mediator to Heaven

The Ascension granted us an eternal mediator to the Heavenly Father: the God-Man Jesus Christ (Heb. 4:14). As the great and eternal High Priest, He prays ceaselessly in the heavenly Holy of Holies for the entire world.

c. The elevation of human nature

Finally, with His Ascension, Christ raised the human nature which was united inseparably with His divinity, as we have mentioned (Eph. 1:20-21). In this glorification of Christ's human nature, the whole human race participates. St. Paul teaches us saying: *"But God, who is rich in mercy, because of His great love with which he loved us, even when we were dead in trespasses, made us alive together with Christ ... and raised us up together, a n d m a d e u s s i t t o g e t h e r i n t h e h e a v e n l y p l a c e s "* (Eph. 2:4-6). *"For the main purpose of the work of Divine Economy was not for us to be left down on earth, but to be raised up to Heaven"* (St. Nicodemus the Athonite, Eortodromion. See also: Jn. 14:3, 17:24; 1Th. 4:17).

14. THE SECOND COMING OF THE LORD

7. "And He shall come again with glory to judge both the living and the dead, Whose Kingdom shall have no end."

Generally

After the Lord's Ascension, the descent of the Holy Spirit and the establishment of the Church followed. At this point, we entered the final stage of the world's history, "eschatology" as it is called. This period will end with the Second Coming of the Lord.

According to Christ's promise, He will come again to judge the world. After the Second Coming we will enter the "Future Age;" endless eternity, which will have two conditions: eternal life (Paradise) or eternal Hell.

As Holy Scripture reveals to us, in the last days, four great events will take place: the end of the world, the Second Coming, the resurrection of the dead, and the Universal Judgment. Let us analyze them.

14.1. THE END OF THE WORLD

Even Science testifies that the world will end one day. According to modern cosmology, the sun will one day cease to exist – the same with all the stars in the heavens. Eventually, all matter will be disintegrated and only a cold and dark universe will remain.

According to Holy Scripture, the world has a beginning and an end. King David the prophet wrote: *"Of old you laid the foundation of the earth, and the heavens are the work of your hands. They will perish, but you will endure. Yes, all of them will grow old like a garment, like a cloak you will change them, and they will be changed."* (Ps. 101/(102): 25-26; see also Matt. 24:35).

The renewal of the universe

Science tells us that the universe will one day return to nothingness; consequently it has no purpose or reason to exist. On the contrary, our Christian faith fills us with hope. It does not allow the world to vanish into a cold darkness. The universe is being driven to destruction, but not to extinction. As mentioned previously, Heaven and earth will be transformed (Ps. 101/(102):25-26). After the end, a new world will dawn, more beautiful, unfading and eternal. St. Peter teaches us saying: *"we... look for new heavens and a new earth"* (2Pt. 3:13; see also Rev. 21:1).

14.2. THE PERIOD BEFORE THE SECOND COMING

The day is unknown

After those startling natural phenomena, the Second Coming of the Lord will take place. The first thing that we have to emphasize is that the day of the Second Coming of the Lord is unknown. The Lord specifically says: *"But of that day and hour no one knows, no, not even the angels of heaven, but my Father only"* (Matt. 24:36). Christ did not reveal when this day would be, in order for us to always be ready.

Let us pay attention to this truth, for every now and then many false prophets announce that the end of the world is near, and they specify dates. We should not believe them.

The *"signs"* which will precede the Second Coming

Our Lord told us of a few events which will take place before the Second Coming. Let us mention them.

a. First, **the Gospel will be preached in all the world** (Matt. 24:14). This has not occurred.

b. **The return of the Israeli nation to Christ.** St. Paul clearly states it (see Rom. 11:25-26; 2Cor. 3:14-16). At present, the Jews deny that the Messiah has come, and they are waiting for Him to appear as a worldly king.

c. **Great apostasy and moral corruption.** After these things, mankind will be ruled by the devil and his followers; and will be led to a great apostasy from God (see 2Ti. 3:1-5).

d. **Persecutions**. At the same time, many persecutions will be declared against the Church; the greatest persecutions which Christianity has ever seen (Matt. 24:9). As a result of these, many Christians' faith will be weakened and they will *betray* their faith (see Matt. 24:10, 12-13).

e. **The appearance of false prophets and the Antichrist**. In addition, many false prophets will appear, who will attempt to deceive those who survive the persecutions (Matt. 24:3-5, 23-24). The last false prophet will be the Antichrist: *"who opposes and exalts himself above all that is called God"* (2Th. 2:3-4). He will fight against the saints on earth and God will allow him to be victorious; he will become a global ruler. All men whose names are not written in the Book of Life will worship him (Rev. 13:5-8).

The reign of the Antichrist will not last long. When the time which God appointed, passes, then *"the Lord will consume [him] with the breath of His mouth and destroy [him] with the brightness of His coming"* (2Th. 2:8).

f. **Various natural and other signs.** Before the Second Coming of the Lord, various signs will take place, e.g. wars, great earthquakes, famines, diseases, etc. (see Matt. 24:6-8, 29).

14.3. THE SECOND COMING OF THE LORD

When evil will have reached its peak; when *"the abomination of desolation"* (Matt. 24:14) places his throne in the Temple of God; when it seems that the Church has been conquered once and for all; and famines, diseases, earthquakes, floods and the darkening of the sun and the moon and the stars will foretell the end of the world – exactly at that moment, the Holy Cross, the sign of the Son of Man, will shine like lightning in the sky, and will foretell the coming of our Great God and Savior Jesus Christ, and will bring salvation to the faithful. (Matt. 24:30).

The Second Coming of the Lord differs from the First (the Incarnation), because whereas then He came as the Savior of the world, at the Second Coming He will come as Judge. Although at the first Coming He came humbly, at the Second Coming He will come *"with power and great glory"* (Matt. 24:30). And another difference: at His first Coming, He came without people noticing Him. At His Second Coming *"every eye will see him;"* (Rev. 1:7) the entire world will see Him. Just as lightning is seen everywhere and by everyone, that's how the Coming of the Lord will be (Matt. 24:27). We stress this, because the Jehovahs' Witnesses say that Christ came "invisibly" in 1914.

14.4. THE UNIVERSAL JUDGMENT

The resurrection of the dead

The first thing that will take place after the glorious appearance of Christ is the resurrection of the dead. All the dead, from Adam until that moment, will be raised. But also all those who will be alive then will change; their bodies will become incorruptible and immortal, just as the bodies of the risen dead (1Cor. 15:51-52). But we will examine this subject when we study the 11th article of the Creed which says: *"I look for the resurrection of the dead."*

The gathering of the entire human race

After the resurrection of the dead, angels will sound the trumpets and gather the entire human race —all the trillions of men who lived in this world— to appear before the righteous Judge and to be judged according to their deeds (Matt. 24:31; Rom. 14:10).

On that day, all our sinful deeds, even our most hidden, will appear as if in a film, before the eyes of all the angels and all mankind – except of course, if we have confessed them.

The criteria

The criteria with which the Judgment will take place, are the Gospel's commandments (Rom. 2:16). Of all the commandments, the chief commandment which Christ will mainly use to judge the world is the commandment of love. This is emphasized in the Bible in the passage concerning the Future Judgment (see Matt. 25:31-46). At that time the Lord will say to the righteous: *"Come, you blessed*

An icon depicting the Second Coming of our Lord

of my Father, inherit the kingdom prepared for you from the foundation of the world. For I was hungry and you gave me food, I was thirsty and you gave me drink, I was a stranger and you took me in, I was naked and you clothed me, I was sick and you visited me, I was in prison and you came to me." He will say the opposite to the sinners. To both the righteous and the sinners, Christ says that all those simple and good deeds that were performed to those who had need of them, were as if they were done to Christ Himself.

But of course love is not enough. In whatever commandment we trespass intentionally, we are trespassing the whole Law (see Jam. 2:10). The Apostle Paul also emphasizes this. (1Cor. 6:9-10).

Remembering Judgment Day

The Old Testament says:*"...remember the time you will die and you will never sin"* (WSir. 7:36). Remembrance of Judgment Day is a rein which holds us from sinning. St. Basil the Great also says that: *"He who continually keeps before his eyes that day and hour when each and every person will be presented to the Judge to give an account for all that he performed; and who contemplates constantly what he will be called to plead, either he won't sin at all, or he will sin very little. For sin originates from the absence within us of the fear of God."*

15. THE ROYAL OFFICE OF CHRIST

"...Whose Kingdom shall have no end"

The Royal Office of the Lord in general

The 7th article of the Holy Creed ends with the words: *"Whose Kingdom shall have no end."* In other words, Christ will rule forever and His Kingdom will exist for eternity (Lk. 1:33).

These words refer to the Royal Office of Christ, according to which Christ as Victor against sin, death and Satan, will rule forever. The Royal Office was also instigated by Christ when He was on earth, but all His glory and authority will appear at His Second Coming.

The Royal Office in Holy Scripture

The Old Testament refers many times to the Royal Office of Christ. The prophets revealed Him as a King who would sit on the throne of David (see Is. 9:7; Ps. 2:6, 2:9). These words of the prophets were misunderstood by the Jews, who awaited the Messiah as an earthly king who would restore the kingdom of Israel and would rule the entire world. But the Kingdom of Christ is not earthly, but heavenly. Christ revealed this to Pontius Pilate saying: *"My kingdom is not of this world"* (Jn. 18:36).

"Blessed is the King who comes in the name of the Lord" (Lk. 19:38) Icon of Palm Sunday

In the New Testament, Christ's Royal authority and glory was manifested many times: in the miracles He performed; during His triumphal entry into Jerusalem; on the Cross where He conquered the devil; during

His descent into Hades; with His Resurrection which conquered death; and at His Ascension where He received the divine glory also as man. Finally, the Royal Office of the Lord will shine at His Second Coming, when He will return to earth with power and great glory, accompanied by a multitude of angels and archangels, and will sit on His glorious throne to judge the entire world as Almighty King.

The Kingdom of Christ will be victorious

Many powerful kingdoms have appeared on earth throughout the centuries. They relied on the power of wealth, the power of the army and the power of weapons and violence. None of them, however, endured the test of time. All of them vanished. They all became like dust scattered by the wind (see Dan. 2:31-45).

Before the end of the world, many other kingdoms will reign. But they will also vanish at one point. Only one kingdom will remain eternal and unshakeable: Christ's Kingdom, His Church. It continues to exist and grow for two thousand years now, despite the persecutions it has endured. And the reason is because the Church is founded upon the rock which is Christ. The devil, sin, death and all the anti-christian powers will one day perish under the scepter of Christ's Kingdom. (1Cor. 15:25).

16. THE HOLY SPIRIT
8. *"And in the Holy Spirit..."*

16.1. THE NATURE OF THE HOLY SPIRIT

Macedonios and the 2nd Oecumenical Synod.

After mentioning the person of our Lord Jesus Christ, the Holy Creed presents to us in the 8th article, the third person of the Holy Trinity, the Holy Spirit. The reason for this was the heresy of Macedonios, patriarch of Constantinople: he taught that the Holy Spirit is not true God but a creation of God. Thus, in the year 381AD the Second Oecumenical Synod took place in Constantinople where it condemned Macedonios' teaching, and professed that the Holy Spirit *is* true God, consubstantial [one in essence] with the Father and the Son. In addition, the Synod added the final five articles of the Holy Creed.

The Holy Spirit is a Person

Firstly, we must emphasize that the Holy Spirit is not an abstract and impersonal force of God, as a few heretics teach, but is a **person**. We see in Holy Scripture that the Holy Spirit s p e a k s to St. Peter (Acts 10:19); d e c i d e s in the Apostolic Synods (Acts 15:28); and elsewhere the Holy Spirit f o r b i d s (Acts 16:6), or w a r n s the Apostles (Acts 20:23), etc. All the above reveal that the Holy Spirit is a person.

The Holy Spirit is true God

The Holy Spirit, however, is not simply a person, as are men or angels. The Holy Spirit is much more than that. The Holy Spirit is perfect **God**, consubstantial with the Father and the Son. The Holy Spirit is the third person of the Holy Trinity. We present a few relevant biblical verses: 1Cor. 3:16, 6:19; 2Cor. 3:16-17; Acts 5:3-4.

"Holy," "Lord," "Life-giver"

The Holy Creed ascribes three characteristics to the Holy Spirit:

a. The Holy Spirit is called *"Holy."* Throughout almost the whole of the New Testament, it is characterized as Holy (see: Lk. 1:35; Matt. 1:20; Jn. 14:26. etc.). But only God is holy, in the absolute meaning of the word. (see: Is. 6:3; Jn. 17:11). Thus the Spirit is God.

b. The Holy Spirit is also called *"Lord":* in other words, He Who rules. The Holy Spirit is *"Lord,"* being All-wise, since *"the Spirit searches all things, yes, the deep things of God"* (1Cor. 2:10). The Holy Spirit is Almighty, since *"by the word of the Lord the heavens were made"* (Ps. 32/(33):6). The Holy Spirit is "all-present" [omnipresent] (Ps.138/(139):7). The Holy Spirit is the source of Truth, since it is the Holy Spirit which enlightens the prophets (2Pt. 1:21). Only God has all of the above attributes.

c. The Holy Spirit is also characterized as *"Life-giver,"* because it gives life. It regenerates man through the Mystery (Sacrament) of Baptism (Jn. 3:5; Tts. 3:5). It forgives the sins of men (Jn. 20:22-23). The Holy Spirit will give us life on the day of the General Resurrection of the dead (Rom. 8:11).

All the above verses indisputably prove the divinity of the Holy Spirit, and that the Holy Spirit is *"Holy," "Lord"* and *"Life-giver."*

Worship and glorification.

Since the Holy Spirit is Lord, Life-giver, consubstantial and equal with the Father and the Son, we consequently say in the Creed: ***"Who with the Father and the Son is together worshipped and glorified."*** We must therefore worship and glorify the Holy Spirit together with the Father and the Son.

16.2. THE PROCEEDING OF THE HOLY SPIRIT
"Who proceedeth from the Father."

The relationship of the Holy Spirit with the Father and the Son

As we have mentioned in chapter two, the Deity has one and only source: the Father. The Son is b e g o t t e n of the Father and the Holy Spirit p r o c e e d s from the Father. For this reason in the Holy Creed we confess: **"And in the Holy Spirit ... Who proceedeth from the Father."**

But what is the relationship between the Holy Spirit and the Son? The Holy Spirit is s e n t by the Son. This has nothing to do with the essence of the persons but with their energies. Both these two fundamental dogmas are based upon the words of Christ, who said: *"But when the Helper comes, Whom I shall s e n d to you from the Father, the Spirit of truth, Who p r o c e e d s from the Father..."* (Jn. 15:26). So we see that the Holy Spirit *"proceeds"* from the Father and is *"sent"* into the world by the Son.

Unfortunately, there was a heresy regarding this important dogma, which became the main reason for a great portion of western Christianity, with the pope as leader, to be cut off from the Church in 1054AD. (The Great Schism). The Papists (Roman Catholics) groundlessly added the phrase *"and from the Son,"* to the Creed; in Latin, the "Filioque" – in other words that the Holy Spirit proceeds not only from the Father but also from the Son.

From the Orthodox viewpoint, the "Filioque" is not a simple theological opinion; it is the prime heresy regarding the Holy Trinity, for it introduces a second source to the Deity —the Son— simultaneous and parallel to the Father.

16.3. THE DESCENT OF THE HOLY SPIRIT

Let us examine a few of the energies of the Holy Spirit in Holy Scripture. The Holy Spirit appears even from the *first* verses of

Genesis, to create the world with the Father and the Son (see Gen. 1:1-2). Later we see the Holy Spirit performing miracles (see Gen. 41:38; Judges 14:6) and inspiring the prophets. This is the "***and spoke by the prophets,***" as mentioned in the Creed.

In the New Testament the Holy Spirit is manifested even more. The Holy Spirit participated in the mystery of the Incarnation of the Son of God (Lk. 1:35). At the Jordan River during Christ's baptism, the Holy Spirit descended *"in the form of a dove"* and affirmed the words of the Father (Matt. 3:17). With the Holy Spirit, the Father anointed the Son as a human, to fulfill His work of redemption (Is. 61:1-2). During the Transfiguration, the Holy Spirit appeared as a bright cloud (see Matt. 17:5).

And so we reach the great day of **Pentecost,** where the Holy Spirit descended and en-lightened the holy Apostles. Pentecost was an ancient Jew-ish feast. Fifty days after their passing through the Red Sea, God gave the Ten Command-ments to Moses on Mount Sinai. God chose the day of this anniversary to send the Holy Spirit to the world and to establish the New Testament with mankind.

The descent of the Holy Spirit at Pentecost

St. Luke the evangelist describes this day, fifty days after Christ's Resurrection, (ten days after His Ascension), where the Apostles were gathered, as follows: *"suddenly there came a sound from heaven, as of a rushing mighty wind, and it filled the whole house where they were sitting. Then there appeared to them divided tongues, as of fire, and one sat upon each of them. And they were all filled with the Holy Spirit and began to speak with other tongues"* (Acts 2:2-4).

But why did the Holy Spirit descend like a rushing, mighty wind? Because as the wind uproots trees; that's how the Holy Spirit blew as a strong wind and uprooted idolatry. The Holy Spirit also appeared as flaming tongues.This reveals His divine nature, because *"the Lord your God is a consuming fire"* (Deut. 4:24). Besides, the tongue would become the instrument by which the Apostles, as "mouths of the Word" would preach the Gospel. And they were flaming, because the tongues of those who preach the Gospel must be "on fire" in order to burn evil: *"a fire which consumes malice"* (St. Gregory the Theologian).

On the day of Pentecost a new period in the history of the world began. On this day the Church was established: the Kingdom of God upon Earth, the Body of Christ, the *"new creation"* (2Cor. 5:17).

16.4. THE WORK OF THE HOLY SPIRIT IN THE CHURCH

In General

The Holy Spirit founded the Church, and remains within it until the end of the world, strengthening and sanctifying its members. Let us examine a few of the energies of the Holy Spirit within the Church.

The Holy Spirit performs and consecrates all the Mysteries (Sacraments) and the acts of Sanctification. It enlightens the prophets to foretell the future. It descended upon the Apostles making them wise preachers of the Gospel. It enlightened the Holy Fathers and Teachers of the Church to oppose the heresies and to express the Orthodox doctrines. The Holy Spirit performs miracles and expels demons. It strengthens the holy martyrs of our Faith, giving them strength to endure the cruel martyrdoms and to remain faithful unto death.

The Holy Spirit reveals the saints of our Church. The saints are the greatest miracle which the Church has to present to the world, because through the grace of the Holy Spirit they are victorious over the devil and the world with its seductions and terrors; they overcome the human passions and their weaknesses; and they become earthly angels, living images of God. For this reason, on the Sunday after Pentecost we celebrate the Sunday of All Saints where we honor all the saints, as fruits of the Holy Spirit.

The care of the Holy Spirit for each of the faithful

We were "sealed" with the Holy Spirit the day we were baptized, and we became a living temple in which God dwells (1Cor. 6:19). It is the Holy Spirit who grants us the internal surety that we are children of God (Gal. 4:6). The Holy Spirit strengthens us in our struggle against sin (Rom. 8:26). The Holy Spirit is the *"Paracletos"* (*"Comforter"* or *"Helper"*) who consoles us and gives us courage and patience every time we encounter sorrows and temptations in life. The Holy Spirit also inspires us to pray (Rom. 8:26), and to worship the heavenly Father in truth (Jn. 4:24). To those who struggle, the Holy Spirit grants great blessings, *"fruits,"* which are: *"love, joy, peace, longsuffering, kindness, goodness, faithfulness, gentleness and self-control"* (Gal. 5:22). Finally, it is the Holy Spirit who will resurrect the lifeless bodies on the day of the General Resurrection (Rom. 8:11).

Our position concerning the Holy Spirit

These and many more are the gifts and blessings which the Holy Spirit grants. That's why the Church especially honors the Holy Spirit. The Church honors the Holy Spirit every year on the "Synaxis of the Holy Spirit," the Monday after Pentecost. The Church also honors the Holy Spirit every day at the service of the 3rd Hour, which is devoted to the Holy Spirit. To the Holy Spirit we address the prayer: *"O Heavenly King, Comforter, the Spirit of truth..."*.

But what should our position be concerning the Holy Spirit? We should not grieve the Holy Spirit (Eph. 4:30) – something we do every time that we sin. We especially sadden and cast the Holy Spirit away when we commit carnal sins. (see Gen. 6:3).

Even more dreadful is **blasphemy against the Holy Spirit;** in other words to ascribe the energies of the Holy Spirit to the devil. This is a sign of man's utter depravity; in reality it is a lack of repentance. Concerning this sin, Christ says: "*every sin and blasphemy will be forgiven men, but the blasphemy against the Spirit will not be forgiven men*" (Matt. 12:31).

The purpose of our life: acquiring the Holy Spirit

A great Russian saint, St. Seraphim of Sarov, emphasized that the purpose of our life is to acquire the Holy Spirit. Everything else we do —prayers, fasting, almsgiving, keeping God's commandments etc.— are nothing more than the *means* to acquire the Holy Spirit. Because, as the apostle Paul mentions: "*For as many as are led by the Spirit of God, these are sons of God*" (Rom. 8:14).

17. THE CHURCH
9. *"In one, Holy, Catholic and Apostolic Church."*

17.1. MEANING, FOUNDATION, PURPOSE, WORK

The meaning of the Church

The 9th article of the Holy Creed refers to the Church. The Greek word for *Church, "Ecclesia,"* means invitation or gathering. According to the Orthodox Christian Faith, the **Church** is all those who are baptized in the name of the Holy Trinity, believe correctly in all the truths which are revealed by God, recognize Jesus Christ as their God and Savior, are nourished by the word of God, are sanctified with the Holy Sacraments, worship God in an orthodox manner, struggle to keep His commandments, and are shepherded by the holy clergy: bishops and priests who are canonically ordained.

The Church as an Ark of salvation

The Founder of the Church

The founder and leader of the Church is our Lord Jesus Christ (see Matt. 16:18). The Church is also the fruit of Christ's Sacrifice on the Cross (Acts 20:28). We could say, however, that the entire

Holy Trinity took part in the creation of the Church, as in the creation of the world.

Consequently, the Church is not a human creation, but a D i - vine Institution.

The founding of the Church

The Church has its origins before the incarnation of Christ (Eph. 2:19-20). But if Christ did not shed His precious Blood on the Cross, the Church would not have existed in its full sense. And just as when Eve was created from Adam's side when he was placed in a trance, likewise the Church was created from Christ's side, with His death. For the water and blood which came out from His side when the soldiers pierced Christ on the Cross, refer to the two fundamental Sacraments; that of Holy Baptism and that of Holy Communion, on which the Church is founded.

But the official establishment of the Church took place on the day of Pentecost, as we have mentioned. This day is considered as the Church's "birthday." As the Holy Spirit created the human body of Christ from the pure blood of the Theotokos on the day of the Annunciation, likewise the Holy Spirit created the spiritual body of Christ, the Church, on the day of Pentecost.

The complete revelation of the Church will take place on the day of the Second Coming of the Lord, when the people of God will achieve full union and communion with the Triune God.

The purpose of the Church

The purpose of the Church is to u t i l i z e Christ's work of redemption and to c o n t i n u e it until the end of the world; i.e. what Christ would have done if He remained on earth, the Church now does. That's why St. Augustine says that *the Church is Christ who is prolonged throughout the ages.*

Consequently, the purpose of the Church is man's salvation by leading him to God.

The means which the Church uses

The Church, as the continuer of Christ's work of redemption, works in the same way which Christ worked when He was on earth, and uses the same means which He used to save man.

a. The first means which the Church uses is teaching: preaching the word of God; because for someone to believe and to be saved he must first hear the Gospel (Rom. 10:17). This is the **teaching work** of the Church.

b. The second means is Divine Grace, which is transmitted through the Holy Sacraments. This is the **sanctifying work** of the Church. And if through the teachings the faithful are enlightened, through the Holy Sacraments they are sanctified.

c. The third means is pastoring to the faithful. The **pastoral work** of the Church, as it is called, is as equally important as the previous two means. The good shepherd (the bishop and priest) will comfort those in pain, will strengthen the faith of those who are stumbling, will run to find those who are in deception, etc.

The pastoral work of the Church also includes **social work**: philanthropy, the creation of community establishments (old people's homes, orphanages, hospitals) etc.

As we can see, the Church continues the threefold work of Christ: the prophetic, that of High-priest and the royal.

17.2. NATURE AND ORDER OF THE CHURCH

Nature of the Church

Just as Christ has two natures, so does the Church: the divine and the human. The divine nature of the Church, mystical and invisible, is Christ, the Holy Spirit and the Divine Grace which sanctifies the faithful. The human nature of the Church, the visible side, is her members, everything that we hear and see: the temple, the holy icons, the holy books, etc.

Each Holy Sacrament or service contains both the visible and invisible element. For example in baptism the visible elements are the water, the oil, etc.; the invisible element is the Holy Spirit which sanctifies the water and the oil.

The Church Militant and the Church Triumphant

The members of the Church, first of all, are the faithful who live on this earth. They comprise of one part of the Church, which is known as the "Church Militant." They are the soldiers of Christ here on earth who fight *the good fight of faith* (1Ti. 6:12). The second part of the Church consists of all those who have departed from this life. They consist of the "Church Triumphant." They are the victorious faithful who are found in God's Kingdom.

There is a close relationship between the two parts of the Church. The angels and the saints in Heaven continuously intercede to God for their brethren who struggle on earth. At the same time, the Church Militant, which is found on earth, honors the saints with temples in their name, feast days, icons and the offering of the Divine Eucharist *in their honor and remembrance.* And for our brothers and fathers who have fallen asleep in the Lord, the Church performs memorial services asking God to give their souls rest.

The clergy and the laity

Just as in the army there are soldiers and officers, likewise in the Church there are the clergy and the laity. The **clergy** is a specific order of people who have received the gift of the priesthood. There are three levels of priesthood: the **deacon**, the **presbyter** (priest) and the **bishop** (*literally:* arch-priest).

The clergy continues the work of Christ and maintains His three offices: the prophetic, by which the clergy teach the people; that of high-priest, by which they bless and sanctify the people; and the royal office, by which they govern and shepherd the people.

The **laymen** receive the blessings of the clergy who they should honor, respect and obey. In addition the laymen participate in the life of the Church and assist the clergy in their work.

The Church's system of government

The Church's system of government is h i e r a r c h i c a l . The clergy are the spiritual leaders of the laity. In every province the bishop holds the pastoral and administrative authority.

The Church's system of government is hieratic (*hieratico*), but not governed hierocratically (*hierocratico*). The purpose of the clergy is to serve, not to be served by the faithful (Matt. 20:28). The perfect example of the good shepherd is given by Christ, who washed the feet of His disciples.

The Oecumenical Synods

The supreme spiritual and administrative authority within the Orthodox Church is the Oecumenical Synod. All the bishops of the Church take part and deal with large and important issues concerning the dogmas, the life and the administration of the Church. The decisions of the Oecumenical Synods are considered God-inspired and infallible, since the Holy Spirit enlightens and guides the participating bishops. The decisions of the Oecumenical Synods are divided into *"hori"* and *canons*. The **hori** are the decisions that relate to the dogmas of faith and the **canons** regulate matters concerning the life, the administration and the ecclesiastical order of the Church.

As we have mentioned above, the Church consists not only of the clergy, but also the laity, the people. Consequently, the faithful contribute to the decisions of the Synods, and many times they form or disqualify the decisions as has occurred at different times in the history of our Church.

17.3. THE ATTRIBUTES OF THE CHURCH
"In one, holy, catholic and apostolic Church."

The Church is ONE

The first element that characterizes the Church is its **unity**, in other words that the Church is O n e and only One. Since Christ who is the Head of the Church is One, then the Church which is the Body of Christ is also One. The various local Churches which we recognize, e.g. the Churches of Greece, Russia, Romania and so forth, are not different bodies, but are different members of the one body. This separation occurred for administrative reasons.

When we say *"one,"* we mean that within the Church there is unity in three basic things: in the Dogmas (the Faith), the ethos (way of life) and the worship.

The Church is HOLY

The second characteristic of the Church is its **holiness, its sanctity**. The Church is h o l y, because its head, Christ, is Holy. And since the head is Holy, the body to which it is united, is made holy.

The Church is holy also, because its purpose is holy. And its purpose is to sanctify its members. The Church has never stopped, nor will stop, creating and producing saints, both known and unknown.

The Church is CATHOLIC

The third characteristic of the Church is that it is **catholic.** When we say that the Church is c a t h o l i c, we mean that its purpose and mission is to spread to the entire world, to preach the Gospel of Christ to all the nations (see Acts 1:8). This missionary work is continued by the Church up unto this day.

In addition, the Church is called catholic referring to its form, because it contains the whole truth. Also, the Church manifests a uniformity throughout; in the entire world its members have the same Orthodox Faith, the same way of life, the same worship, and the same ecclesiastical administration.

Finally, we must emphasize that only the Orthodox Church is catholic, because only the Orthodox Church upholds the universal elements of the Church. The western catholic (papist) church is wrongly called "catholic" and wrongly "church," because it did not preserve the universal elements of the Church, since it has fallen into many false teachings and doctrines.

The Church is APOSTOLIC

The fourth characteristic of the Church is that it is **apostolic**. The Church is a p o s t o l i c , because it was established *"upon the foundations of the apostles"* (Eph. 2:20). Also it contains and preserves pure and undefiled, the apostolic teachings.

Furthermore, the Church is apostolic, for it links back to the apostles through unbroken a p o s t o l i c s u c c e s s i o n . In other words, the bishops of our Church are successors of the apostles. The apostles ordained bishops, and those bishops ordained other bishops and so on, until we reach todays bishops. This link is proven historically and is preserved in the historical bishops' catalogues in each local Church.

The heretics do not have apostolic succession. Their history begins from the time their leaders appeared, whereas the true Church has its beginning from the holy apostles. The heretics are plants which were not planted by God the Father (see Matt. 15:13).

17.4 WHICH IS THE TRUE CHURCH?

A question

In the Creed, we confess that we believe in "one, holy, catholic and apostolic Church." Which, however, is this Church? In these times the Christian world is in a state of confusion. A myriad of christian communities and confessions, with great differences between them, call themselves "churches." We hear of the "Catholic Church," the "Anglican Church," the "Lutherans" and so on. Which of all these contains the truth? Which is the **one** true Church of Christ, the ark of salvation? This important question needs to be examined with care, because our salvation depends on the answer.

A Monastery of Mt. Athos, Greece

Orthodoxy upholds the Faith without change

If someone studies all these denominations, they will find that Orthodoxy and only Orthodoxy has remained faithful to the Truth which Christ and the apostles handed down to us. Only Orthodoxy upholds the dogmas and decisions of the Oecumenical Synods unchanged, and has remained steadfast to the Faith which the Church had up until the schism. And since then it has neither added nor subtracted the smallest thing from this Faith. On the other hand, as we will see below, all the other denominations changed the truthfulness of the Faith.

In addition, the Orthodox Church has apostolic succession. That is, its clergy consists of the continuation of an unbroken chain which has its beginning with the apostles. Let us look, however, at the other Christian denominations.

The Roman Catholics (The Papacy)

Reflection in History (Historical Retrospection)

It is known from ecclesiastical history that until the 11th C the whole Christian world was united. In 1054AD the Great **Schism** occurred. A great portion of the western Christian world, with their leader as the pope of Rome, cut themselves off from the Eastern Church and constitutes the so-called "Roman Catholic Church," or more correctly, the Latin or Papist church.

The reasons for the Schism were a) theological (the addition of the Filioque to the Creed) b) ecclesiastical (the primacy of the pope and his conceited desire to control the whole Church) and c) political (the west [the Franks] wanted to show that they could create their own empire).

After the Schism, the Latins drew even further away from ecclesiastical tradition and deviated into a host of theological and ecclesiastical errors.

The erroneous beliefs of the Latins

Let us see some of the erroneous beliefs of the Latins.

a. The **Filioque**. This was discussed in chapter 16.2.

b. The **primacy and infallibility of the pope**. They uphold the belief that the pope, as successor to the apostle Peter, is the representative of Christ on earth, and is the visible head of the church. However, the apostle Peter, aside from founding the church in Rome —and it is not certain that he did this— founded churches in other places as well.

In the 13th C the theory that the pope is infallible was formulated. That is, when he sits on his throne and speaks regarding matters of faith, everything the pope says is considered infallible and it benefits the church to accept it. He is considered to be above even the Oecumenical Synods. However in the history of the Church, many popes were heretical and condemned by the

Synods, therefore they are not infallible. Only God is infallible.

c. **The created energies of God and created grace.** The papists do not accept that the energies of God are uncreated. For them, the divine energies such as Divine Grace, are created. This teaching has devastating consequences in the life of a Christian, because if Divine Grace is created, man cannot reach holiness and *theosis* (deification).

d. Another erroneous belief is the teaching concerning **the merits of the saints**. According to this teaching, in their lifetime the saints performed more good deeds than what was required for them to be saved. Their extra good deeds can be used by the pope who can allocate them to others who lack good deeds.

This theory is completely at odds with Holy Scripture. We are all saved by the grace and mercy of God. No saint performed or could have performed more than what was required for their salvation (see Php. 3:12).

e. The Latins even teach that between Paradise and Hell exists an intermediate state called **Purgatory**. They say that the souls of those who died without having time to confess, although they desired to; or those who didn't complete the penance that their spiritual father gave them, go to Purgatory. There they are tormented for a certain amount of time and after that they go to Paradise. The amount of time they are in Purgatory can be reduced if the pope grants them the so-called "*Indulgencias*" which the relatives of the dead person can buy.

However this intermediate state is not mentioned anywhere in the Holy Gospel. Only Heaven and Hell exist (see Matt. 25:46 etc.).

f. In 1854 the Latins introduced the "dogma" of the **Immaculate Conception** of the Theotokos, which says that the Virgin Mary was born without Ancestral Sin. In 1950 they added the "dogma" concerning the **Ascension** of the Theotokos, where they state that the Virgin Mary was raised to heaven without first knowing death. Both these beliefs are wrong.

g. **Innovations to the Sacraments**. From the 14th C the "Catholic Church" abolished the triple immersion into water that occurs at baptism, and replaced it with sprinkling.

For the Sacrament of **Holy Communion** they use unleavened bread. From the 12th C onwards, they commune the laity using only the "body" (wafers) and not the "blood" of Christ, despite Christ's commandment *"Drink from it, all of you..."* (Matt. 26:27).

The other Sacraments have also been altered, as well as fasting rules etc.

The condemnation of the Latins

The Latin church has been condemned at different times by various Synods. The third and fourth Oecumenical Synods (in 431AD and 451AD) condemned as a heretic, whoever changed the Symbol of Faith (the Creed). The Latins changed it when they added the Filioque. The Synod which St. Photios the great convened in 879-880 condemned the heresy of the Filioque. The Synod convened by St. Gregory Palamas in 1351 condemned the heresy of "created grace." In later years the patriarchs of the East repeatedly condemned the Papacy in Synods which occurred in Constantinople (1722, 1727, 1755, 1838, 1848, 1895).

Protestantism

Generally

In 1517AD the protestant movement broke out as a negative reaction to the pope making innovations using his supremacy; the riches gained from his *"Indulgencias;"* and the degeneration of ethics, amongst other things. The movement quickly predominated, and a large portion of Europe segmented from the Latins.

Unfortunately however, although Protestantism began as a just protest against the Latins, in the end it found itself at the opposite extreme. It proceeded with innovations which removed it even further from the Truth.

The erroneous beliefs of the Protestants

The first error of the Protestants is that they discard **Holy Tradition**. They only keep Holy Scripture, which each person interprets as they wish. As a result of this, they are continuously fragmented and create many different "churches." Today the approx. three hundred million protestants who exist in the world, are broken up into hundreds of groups, which contain huge dogmatic differences between them. Let us examine some of their erroneous beliefs.

For a start, they overemphasize preaching the word of God and underestimate or even completely discard the Holy Sacraments.

They discard **Confession**, teaching that it is enough simply to confess our sins during prayer and they will be forgiven. The Lord Himself, however, appointed the holy apostles to forgive sins (see John 20:22-23) and the apostles transmitted this grace to their successors, the bishops and priests.

Concerning the Sacrament of Holy Communion, during which we commune the Body and Blood of Christ, in accordance with the Lord's explicit commandment "*Take, eat; this is My body.... Drink from it, all of you. For this is My blood...*" (Matt. 26:26-28) the protestants consider that it is a simple rite during which we remember Christ's sacrifice, and that Holy Communion isn't really the Body and Blood of Christ but is bread and wine which simply symbolizes the Body and Blood of Christ.

Most protestant denominations have completely abolished the **priesthood**. Instead of priests they have pastors, who are mostly preachers of the divine word. We know, however, that in the Old Testament, God Himself appointed priests and bishops to offer the gifts and sacrifices on behalf of the people (see Ex.

29:4-10; Lev. 8:1-36). In the New Testament the first bishops were the holy apostles who later transmitted the grace of priesthood to others. In the apostolic Church we encounter all three ranks of priesthood (see Php. 1:1; Acts 20:17-18; Tit. 1:5; Rev. 2:3 and more).

The protestants uphold that good works are not necessary for our salvation. Man, they say, is saved **only by the grace of God**. It is enough only to believe in the sacrifice of Christ. Of course faith is essential for our salvation, but it is not enough. We also need good works because "faith without works is dead" (Jam. 2:26). Both Christ and the holy apostles emphasize the importance of good works (see Matt. 7:21; 16:27; Rom. 2:6; I Cor. 13:2, Jam. 2:14; Rev. 22:12).

In contrast to the Latins, who overly revere the Virgin Mary, the protestants do not honor her at all. Some of them deny her ever-virginity and maintain that she bore other children besides Christ. However this is not so. The Virgin Mary is *"full of grace"* and *"blessed among women"* (Lk. 1:28), since she was vouched worthy to give birth to the God-Man Christ. She gave birth without knowing a man, *"of the Holy Spirit,"* as the angel revealed to Joseph (Matt. 1:20). Panagia did not have other children. The so-called *"brothers"* of Christ (Matt. 13:55-56) were the children of Joseph from his first wife.

The protestants **do not honor the saints**, nor do they have feast days for them. They do not pray to the saints, they pray only to Christ. Holy Scripture, however, refers to many situations where holy people such as Abraham, Moses, the prophets, the apostles and more, prayed for others and their prayers were heard (see Gen. 20:7; Num. 11:1-3; Acts 9:36-42; Jam. 5:16; Rev. 5:8 and more). Therefore, we may ask for the intercession of the saints.

Besides these errors, the protestants reject the use of **icons**, they don't believe that **Holy Water** (*Agiasmos)* has grace, they deny the benefits that the **memorial services** offer to the reposed souls and much more. Finally, they have a very strange theory concerning the "**Invisible Church**" which, as they say, consists of holy members of all the visible "churches."

Conclusions

As we mentioned, today there are hundreds of protestant denominations. Some of them, such as the Anglicans, ordain women priests and perform homosexual "weddings." It is obvious that all of these denominations do not have any relation with the Faith and ethos which Christ, the holy Apostles and the Holy Fathers transmitted to us.

After this brief analysis, we reach the conclusion that the One, Holy, Catholic and Apostolic Church which Christ instituted, which the Holy Creed mentions, is **our Orthodox Church**; the Church which still believes today, what it believed twenty centuries ago. This is also confessed by many of the heterodox who have become members of the Body of Christ through baptism into the Orthodox Church.

18. THE MEANS OF SANCTIFICATION OF THE CHURCH

10. *"I acknowledge one baptism for the remission of sins."*

18.1. GENERALLY, CONCERNING THE MEANS OF SANCTIFICATION

The Church's means of sanctification

The 10th article of the Holy Creed refers to Holy Baptism, by which man becomes a member of the Church. This provides us with a reason to speak about the means of sanctification which the Church uses.

St. John the Evangelist mentions that the *"Grace and **truth** came [into the world] through Jesus Christ"* (Jn. 1:17). These words reveal the two means which Christ used for the salvation of the world: Grace and truth. The Church uses the same two means for the work of sanctification. The truth is spread by **preaching** the divine word, whereas grace is granted through the **Holy Sacraments**.

Both are equally needful for man's salvation. With preaching, the soul is enlightened, and through the Holy Mysteries it is sanctified. The Gospel and the holy chalice are the two means by which the Church offers salvation to the faithful.

Divine Grace and its importance

In the 10th chapter we spoke concerning the importance and power of the word of God, where we mentioned the prophetical work of Christ. Let us now examine the second means of sanctification: Divine Grace. The Church is not only the preacher of Truth; it is also the treasury of Divine Grace. And just as without rain, seeds planted in the earth cannot sprout; likewise without Divine Grace, the seed of truth cannot grow nor bear fruit.

But, what is Divine Grace? It is the sanctifying energy of God which originates from the Cross of Christ. With Divine Grace the world's salvation is actualized within the Church.

Divine Grace is a gift of God which is offered to all men (1Ti. 2:4). However no one is compelled to accept it.

18.2. THE HOLY MYSTERIES / SACRAMENTS OF THE CHURCH

The Holy Sacraments

Divine Grace is transmitted to men in many and various ways, but mainly it is transmitted by the Holy Sacraments of the Church. And what are the Holy Sacraments? The *Holy Sacraments* are the sacred ceremonies which Christ Himself or the apostles instituted, and in which Divine Grace is transmitted to the faithful in a supernatural way.

What are the Holy Sacraments

There are seven Holy Sacraments:

1. H o l y B a p t i s m , which renews man, and makes him a member of the Church and inheritor of eternal blessedness.

2. C h r i s m a t i o n . It is performed together with Holy Baptism and grants the gifts of the Holy Spirit to the person who is being baptized.

3. H o l y E u c h a r i s t / Holy Communion, which nourishes the faithful with the Body and Blood of Christ and grants him eternal life.

4. R e p e n t a n c e and C o n f e s s i o n , which grant forgiveness of sins.

5. M a r r i a g e , which blesses and sanctifies the union of man and woman.

The seven Holy Mysteries of the Church

6. P r i e s t h o o d, which appoints the spiritual shepherds of the Church (deacons, presbyters and bishops).

7. H o l y   U n c t i o n, which heals the ill.

Baptism, Chrismation, Holy Communion and Confession are **compulsory** Sacraments. Marriage, Priesthood and Holy Unction are **optional**. Holy Communion, Confession and Marriage are repeatable (Marriage up to three times). Baptism, Holy Chrismation and Priesthood are not repeatable.

As we see, man's salvation is impossible without the Grace of the Holy Mysteries. Good deeds are not enough. It is essential for us to be continuously sanctified by the Holy Mysteries of the Church. Some people who, out of ignorance say that "it is not essential to go to church, it is enough just to be a good person and God will take you to Paradise," should take note of this. This is a great deception and trap of the devil. Besides our good deeds, the Divine Grace which is granted through the Holy Mysteries of the Church, is absolutely necessary.

How should we approach the Holy Sacraments?

Although the Holy Sacraments act regardless of the moral condition of the priest who celebrates them, their results depend on the spiritual condition of the faithful who participate in them. For Divine Grace to be effective on someone, he must be properly prepared to receive it.

The apostle Paul teaches us, concerning Holy Communion, that whoever partakes of the Body and Blood of the Lord unworthily, brings condemnation upon himself (see 1Cor. 11:29). The Holy Sacraments do not grant Divine Grace magically.

18.3. THE SACRAMENT OF HOLY BAPTISM

The Sacrament of Holy Baptism generally

Baptism is the gateway by which man enters into the Church and officially becomes a member and heir of the eternal promises.

It is the beginning and the source of all the Holy Sacraments, because whoever is baptized immediately receives the right to participate in all the other Sacraments.

The foundation of Christian Baptism

Holy Baptism is a God-instituted Sacrament. It was founded and delivered to us by Christ Himself. Concerning the importance of baptism, Christ revealed to His disciple Nicodemus, that *"unless one is born of water* 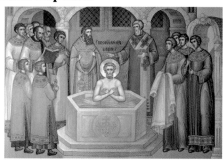 (Baptism) *and the Spirit, he cannot enter the kingdom of God"* (Jn. 3:3-5).

Also, a little before Christ's Ascension into the Heavens, He explicitly commanded His disciples to *"go therefore and make disciples of all the nations, b a p t i z i n g them in the name of the Father and of the Son and of the Holy Spirit"* (Matt. 28:19). The apostles did this, and the Church also continues to do it up until this day.

The Gifts of Holy Baptism

A. **The forgiveness of sins.** St. Paul teaches us that during baptism man participates in the death and resurrection of Christ; he dies to sin and is raised together with Christ (Rom. 6:3-5). During baptism the *"old man,"* the man of sin, is put to death (Rom. 6:6; Eph. 4:22; Col. 3:9). The sanctified water of the baptismal font washes away the Ancestral Sin and all personal sins of the one who is baptized. Baptism is the spiritual bath which cleanses the soul and makes it *"whiter than snow"* (Ps. 50/(51): 9).

B. **Rebirth and regeneration.** According to the Lord's words to Nicodemus which we mentioned above (Jn. 3:3-5), at baptism a supranatural birth takes place. This regeneration initiates man into a new life. With baptism, man regains the former beauty which he had before the Ancestral Sin. The image of God which was soiled because of sin is cleansed, and the soul shines with divine glory.

Infant Baptism and Baptism of Necessity

In the ancient Church, baptism was performed at a mature age and after a series of lessons, with sufficient catechism. Later, the Church established **infant baptism**, for two reasons. Firstly, for the child to be able to receive Holy Communion and the blessings of the Church from infancy; and secondly, in order for it not to depart from this world unbaptized if it were do die at an early age.

However, infant baptism was established by the Church with the presupposition that the parents would be conscientious and devoted Christians. In addition, a responsible person would have to be officially accountable for the child's learning about its faith. This person is known as the g o d p a r e n t .

In the case when an infant's life is in danger before it is baptized, then **aerial baptism** can be performed by any Orthodox Christian in the following way: They elevate the infant three times in the air saying: *"The servant of God (name) is baptized in the name of the Father* (1st elevation) *and of the Son* (2nd elevation) *and of the Holy Spirit* (3rd elevation). *Amen."* The infant is then considered baptized.

Confession, a Second Baptism

Baptism i s n o t r e p e a t a b l e . Just as a natural birth takes place only once, likewise baptism, which is a spiritual birth, is performed only once.

But what happens if someone sins after their baptism? The Church, following the teachings and the example of the Lord, appointed a second baptism: the Mystery of Repentance and Confession. The Christian can approach this Sacrament every time they sin, and once they have confessed their sins with repentance, they receive forgiveness of sins.

19. THE RESURRECTION OF THE DEAD

11. *"I look for the Resurrection of the dead"*

19.1. DEATH

The meaning of death

The 11ᵗʰ article of the Symbol of Faith (the Creed) says: *"I look for the Resurrection of the dead."* Before we elaborate on this important subject of the resurrection of the dead, we will deal with the event that preludes it: death.

Death is the separation of the soul from the body, which has as a result, the deadening and decay of the body. Death is something that will happen to everyone, no one is exempted from it. But although death is the most certain event in our life, the hour of our death is the most uncertain thing in our life.

St. Sisoes at the grave of Alexander the Great

And the reason God has hidden this from us, is in order to keep us alert and to always be ready for our departure.

Why death?

Man was not created by God to die, but to live eternally. Later, death entered his life as the result of sin. Therefore, death is an unnatural situation. That's why every person dreads death.

But the philanthropy of God lies behind death. He consented to death existing *"in order that evil will not become eternal"* (St. Gregory the Theologian).

The hour of death and the taxing of souls

And we come to the hour of death. St. John Chrysostom teaches that *"at that time, the soul does not want to depart from the body and moves deeper into it and is afraid and terrified"* (Homily II On the Rich Man and Lazarus). Death is especially frightening for sinners (Ps. 33/(34):22). On the contrary, the death of the righteous is quiet, peaceful and calm.

After their departure from their bodies, all the souls are attacked by evil spirits who demand the souls be given to them. At that frightful time, the soul is scrutinized intensively for its deeds by the demons, and a harsh struggle between the angels and demons takes place as to who will take the soul. The demons accuse the souls of their sins, whereas the angels present their good deeds (alms-giving, fasting, prayers etc.). The evil spirits are called *telonia* (customs-demons).

The teaching concerning the existence of the toll-houses is supported by the words Christ spoke a little before His Passion: *"In a short time, the ruler of this sinful world, the devil, is coming; he will examine me, but he won't find anything in me that belongs to him"* (see Jn. 14:30).

The existence of the toll-houses is also accepted by many holy Fathers of the Church.

If in the end the soul was found to have lived *"piously and in a way pleasing to God,"* the angels receive it and it *"goes into that ineffable joy"* of eternal life. But, if the soul is found to have lived *"carelessly and prodigally,"* then the good angels abandon it with profound regret and *" it is received by those dark demons so that they may fling it with much malevolence into the prisons of Hades"* (St. Cyril of Alexandria, "On the Exodus of the Soul, and On the Second Coming" P.G. 77, 1073C-1076D).

19.2. LIFE AFTER DEATH

The very significant parable of "the Rich Man and Lazarus" gives us much information about the life of the souls in the other world (see Lk. 16:22-31). This parable gives us information on the following subjects:

1. **How and where are the souls transferred to after death?** The souls of the righteous are carried *"by the angels"* *"to Abraham's bosom,"* in other words to Paradise. On the contrary, the souls of the sinners who have not repented are taken by the demons *"to the place of torments,"* in other words, to Hades.

2. **How do the souls live in the afterlife?** The condition in which the soul enters after death, and remains there until the Second Coming, is called the "Middle State." It is a state of anticipation and the soul experiences a foretaste of that which it will enjoy in full after the Second Coming. The souls of the righteous are happy and rejoice, whereas the souls of the sinners are tormented and suffer.

3. **It is impossible to move from one condition to the other.** The soul of a righteous person cannot go to Hades, neither can the soul of a condemned person go to Paradise. For as Abraham said, between the two conditions there is *"a great chasm."*

4. **The souls recognize each other.** The Rich Man recognized Lazarus; he also recognized Abraham, who lived many centuries previously. Consequently, the souls recognize each other, and indeed, to a greater degree than previously.

5. **The souls remember us and pray for us.** We see that the Rich Man remembered his brothers and was concerned for them. Consequently, our departed friends and relatives think of us and pray for us. In particular, the saints pray and intercede for us, and above all the Ever-Virgin Mary, the Theotokos.

Reincarnation

According to this theory, after death the souls re-enter other bodies of humans or even animals! The Church rejects the theory of reincarnation, considering it a delusion of the devil. St. Paul teaches us that a man dies *"once"* (Heb. 9:27) and then judgment follows. Besides, if a soul were to have passed through many bodies, when the General Resurrection takes place, to which of all the bodies will it return? But, what will happen with the rest of the bodies? With which soul will *they* be raised? This theory of reincarnation is supported by many ancient races and philosophers such as Plato. Today it is a teaching of Buddhism, Hinduism, Theosophy and Spiritism.

Communication with the souls, i.e. Mediums

Another delusion of the devil is **mediumism.** Mediumism is the communication with the world of evil spirits, which is accomplished through people who are called **mediums.** The medium supposedly calls upon the dead with whom they speak and transfer messages to the dead person's relatives. In addition the relatives themselves can supposedly see their beloved and speak with them.

The Christian Faith does not accept these phenomena, because immediately after death the souls go directly to the "middle state" and do not return to earth. The voice of those who passed away or the image which appears is clearly a work of Satan. The demons can perfectly imitate the voice of our beloved or take on their image. The mediums are undeniably instruments of the devil.

19.3. MEMORIAL SERVICES

Prayers for the reposed. Memorial Services

Just as the souls of those who have fallen asleep pray for us, likewise we pray for them. From the early Christian years, the Church established special **prayers** for the departed souls. It also established the **Memorial Services,** which are performed on specific days.

Kollyva for the reposed

The Church celebrates the Memorial Services on the following days: On the third day after death in honor of Christ who rose on the third day, and to whom we pray to forgive the souls of the reposed; on the ninth day in honor of the nine angelic orders, to whom we pray to intercede for the soul's rest; and on the fortieth day for the Ascension of the Savior which took place forty days after the Resurrection. Following this we have the Memorial Services performed three months, six months and nine months after death, and finally, the annual Memorial Services.

The Church also established **All-souls day** twice yearly, on the Saturday before Meat-fare Sunday and the Saturday before Pentecost, to pray for all those who departed from this life without funerals or memorial services (e.g. those who were lost at sea, in the desert, at war, etc.), and invites us to pray for their repose.

At the Memorial Service, boiled wheat mixed with other fruit and nuts is offered (*kollyva*). The *kollyva* contains a most didactic symbolism. As the wheat falls on the earth, decays and decomposes, and then it sprouts a new plant; likewise, when a person dies, his body is buried in the earth, decays and decomposes, but one day it will be resurrected, more beautiful, and will acquire a new life, imperishable and eternal.

The benefits of the Memorial services

Do the souls receive any benefit from the Memorial Services? After death the souls cannot change the condition they find themselves in. However, the Memorial Services offer them some kind of comfort. In Holy Scripture we see that prayers are offered for those who have fallen asleep, in order for them to find mercy on Judgment Day (see 2Mc. 12:40-43; 2Tim. 1:18). Even the Holy Fathers of the Church teach us that the souls receive benefit through our prayers, the Memorial Services, and especially when they are commemorated during the Divine Liturgy. How much the souls are benefited and helped, however, we do not know.

Also, the souls receive great benefit from the alms-giving we offer in their name.

All that we do for the souls of our beloved, also benefit us personally, because they are deeds of love and God blesses them. They also strengthen our faith in the future life and keep alight the hope of us meeting again.

19.4. THE RESURRECTION OF THE DEAD

The foundation of the Church

Let us examine the important dogma concerning the resurrection of the dead. This great truth is proclaimed by the 11th article of the Holy Creed, which states: *"I look for the Resurrection of the dead."* In other words, I await, with desire and longing, the resurrection of the dead. The belief in the resurrection of the dead, together with belief in the Resurrection of Christ consists of the fundamental basis of the Church and the central theme of the teachings of the holy Apostles.

The Apostle Paul develops this great theme in the 15th chapter of his 1st letter to the Corinthians, saying amongst other things that *"if there is no resurrection of the dead, then Christ is not risen."* (1Cor. 15:13). And if Christ is not risen, then our faith is futile and empty, and we who have placed our hope in Christ, are the most wretched and pitiable of all men.

But, "no!" the apostle Paul continues: Christ is risen from the dead and with His Resurrection He became the *"firstfruits of those who have fallen asleep"* (1Cor. 15:14-20), i.e. the first amongst the dead who rose and continues to live (Rom. 6:9). Christ's Resurrection will be followed by the General Resurrection. Since Christ who is the Head, rose, His Body —the Church, i.e. all the faithful— will also be resurrected.

The meaning of the Resurrection of the dead

What exactly do we mean when we say the *resurrection of the dead*? According to divine revelation: a) the body which was buried in the earth and which dissolved, will be recreated. In other words the body's material elements will reunite and will create a body once again. b) The soul, which was separated from the body by death, will return and will be reunited with it. c) The body will come alive and will be resurrected incorruptible and immortal in order to live eternally.

Objections

This great truth concerning the resurrection of the dead is very difficult for a person to accept, because it runs contrary to human logic and experience. How is it possible for the body that decays in the earth and dissolves, to rise? We answer:

1. The event of the resurrection of the dead will not be an act of human strength. It will be an accomplishment of the A l - m i g h t i n e s s o f G o d . For with God, nothing is impossible (Lk. 1:37). Just as God created the universe by His almighty word, and indeed without pre-existing matter, that's how He will now raise the dead bodies.

2. G o d ' s r i g h t e o u s n e s s d e m a n d s it. *"For we see many righteous being treated unjustly, whereas many sinners and un-righteous people prosper with riches and luxuries. There must be a resurrection, because God is righteous 'and He rewards those who diligently seek Him' (Heb. 11:6) ... And since the soul performed good and evil together with the body, together they will receive both the rewards and the punishments"* (St. John of Damascus, On the Resurrection 27 [100], p. 444 [in Greek]).

3. The body has been sanctified by baptism, it has been nour-ished with Holy Communion and has become the *"temple of God"* (1Cor. 3:16). *"How, therefore, can the body give in to mortality and not share in life, since it is nourished from the Body and Blood of the Lord?"* (St. Irenaeus, Migne 7, 1028-29 [in Greek]).

Testimonies from Holy Scripture

The reality of the resurrection of the dead is not a human invention. God Himself has revealed it to us in Holy Scripture.

1. Testimonies from the Old Testament.

The prophet Isaiah proclaimed that: *"the dead shall rise up; and those in the tombs shall arise."* (Is. 26:19). Reference is also made in the book of II Maccabees, where one of the seven heroic brothers said to the tyrant who was torturing him: *"I received these* [bodily members] *from heaven and because of His laws I* [now] *disregard them, and from Him I hope to get them back again."* (2Mc.7:11). But the most characteristic text concerning the resurrection of the dead is the prophecy of Ezekiel. It is a vision which the prophet saw, where he found himself in a plain which was full of human bones. By God's commandment he prophesied to them, and the bones assembled themselves, were covered with flesh and finally came back to life (Ezk. 37:1-14).

Prophet Ezekiel's vision

2. Testimonies from the New Testament.

a. The first and main testimony is that of Christ Himself who assured us saying: *"The hour is coming in which all who are in the graves will hear His voice and come forth – those who have done good, to the resurrection of life, and those who have done evil, to the resurrection of condemnation"* (Jn. 5:28-29).

b. The second is that of the apostle Paul who says: *"For if we believe that Jesus died and rose again, likewise we must believe that God, for those who have died with faith in Jesus, will raise them and will take them into the eternal life with Him"* (see 1Th. 4:14).

c. The apostle Paul also speaks extensively about the resurrection of the dead in the 15th chapter of his first epistle to the Corinthians.

And one more proof. Holy Scripture is filled with prophesies. Most of them have been fulfilled to the letter. This guarantees us that the prophesies which refer to the resurrection of the dead, the Second Coming and eternal life, will also be fulfilled.

Testimonies from nature

Besides Holy Scripture, God allowed this great mystery of the resurrection of the dead to be manifested by examples from nature. Besides the example of the seed of wheat which we have already mentioned, St. Cyril of Jerusalem adds: *"It is winter now. The trees are as dead. Where are the leaves of the fig tree or the vine leaves? In spring however, the trees will come back to life, they will be clothed again with their leaves as if they were resurrected from the grave. Because God knows your disbelief, for this reason every year He repeats the resurrection through these natural phenomena, in order for you to believe that since this occurs to things not having a soul, it will also take place amongst the logical creations who have a soul"* (Catechesis XVIII, 6-7 [in Greek]).

How will the Resurrection of the dead take place?

Let us now examine how the apostle Paul describes the resurrection of the dead. In his first epistle to the Thessalonians, he writes: *"The Lord Himself will descend from heaven with a shout, with the voice of an archangel, and with the trumpet of God. And the dead in Christ will rise first. Then we who are alive and remain shall be caught up together with them in the clouds to meet the Lord in the air. And thus we shall always be with the Lord"* (1Th. 4:16-17).

And elsewhere: *"For the trumpet will sound, and the dead will be raised incorruptible, and we shall be changed. For this corruptible must put on incorruption, and this mortal must put on immortality"* (1Cor. 15:51-55).

Here also we notice that the resurrection of the dead will take place at the Second Coming of the Lord. And while the dead will be risen *"incorruptible,"* those who will still be alive will have their bodies changed; their bodies will also become incorruptible and immortal, like those who were resurrected.

What will the resurrected bodies be like?

As we can conclude from the holy texts, the resurrected bodies will be as they are now, but will have different properties. They will be incorruptible and immortal. They will not have the physical needs that they have now. They will not hunger, or thirst, or feel pain; they will not become ill, nor will they reproduce (see Matt. 22:30).

All the bodies will rise. But as St. Cyril observes, they will not all be the same. The righteous will receive a *"heavenly"* body (1Cor. 15:40), so that it can accompany the angels. It will be glorious and bright, as was the Body of Christ after His Resurrection (see Php. 3:20-21). On the contrary, although the bodies of the sinners will also be resurrected —since the resurrection is a gift common to the nature of man— they will be dark and ugly. They will also be incorruptible and immortal; however not to enjoy eternal blessedness, but to suffer the eternal punishments and torments.

The belief in the resurrection of the dead

St. Cyril of Jerusalem notes that this belief and hope in the resurrection of the dead is the *"root of all good deeds."* Whoever believes that his body will be resurrected, takes care to preserve it pure and undefiled. And as a garment of the soul, he does not soil it with carnal sins and other filth (Catechesis XVIII).

On the contrary, he who does not believe in the resurrection of the dead and the consequences, will wallow in the mud of sin, without any restrictions. St. Paul teaches that *"if the dead do not rise, then let us practice that which the unbelievers and materialists say: 'Let us eat and drink, for tomorrow we shall die'"* (see 1Cor. 15:32).

20. THE FUTURE LIFE TO COME

12. "And the life of the age to come."

Introduction

After the resurrection of the dead and the Universal Judgment, "the life of the age to come" will follow. The first characteristic of the future age is that it is e t e r n a l (Lk. 1:33); it will have no end. It will also be unchangeable. After the Final Judgment, man's condition will not be able to change. Finally, eternal life will be in t w o   f o r m s, i.e. there will be two completely different forms of eternity. For the righteous there will be eternal glory and blessedness —**Paradise**— whereas for the impious and unrepentant there will be eternal condemnation and torment: **Hell**.

20.1. HELL

Does Hell exist?

Many people maintain that Hell does not exist. They say that it is impossible for the God of love to have prepared Hell, into which He will throw His creations to be tortured, and indeed for eternity. What answer can we give to this?

1. For a start, the concept of Hell and Paradise is not a human invention. Heaven and Hell are truths which Christ Himself revealed to us. His words are very clear. After the Second Coming, two conditions will exist: *"the kingdom"* —Paradise— which God has prepared for the righteous; and the *"everlasting fire"* —Hell— which was prepared for the devil and his angels, and where sinners will find themselves (see Matt. 25:34 & 41). Consequently, whosoever doubts the existence of Hell presents God *"as a liar"* (St. John Chrysostom).

2. The view that God in His goodness cannot punish men, etc., is in fact nothing more than a sly trap of the devil. *"The evil one knows that the fear of Hell is a bridle which holds back the*

soul and restrains it from evil. He therefore tries in every way to remove it from us, in order to easily throw us into the abyss" (St. John Chrysostom).

An icon depicting hell

Besides, as we can see from history, God does not only threaten, but also carries out His threats when repentance does not exist. We recall the Great Flood, the destruction of Sodom and Gomorrah, etc. *"If all these people were punished, why should we be excluded? Would it not be illogical, since we have committed so many mortal sins? The matter is simple. We are not punished now, because the future punishment awaits us"* (St. John Chrysostom).

3. The existence of Hell and Paradise is required by G o d ' s r i g h t e o u s n e s s. *"When you see murderers, thieves, robbers, crooks etc. remaining unpunished, whether you want to or not, you have to accept the existence of Hell, because God is not unrighteous and does not discriminate. God would be unjust if He left so many sinners unpunished and so many righteous to be tortured"* (St. John Chrysostom).

What is Hell?

But what is Hell? It is something that cannot be described in words. Our Lord, in order to portray Hell, used the most frightful images of this world. He calls Hell *"everlasting fire"* (Matt. 18:8), *"furnace of fire... wailing and gnashing of teeth"* (Matt. 13:42), *"outer darkness"* (Matt. 25:30), and elsewhere *"where their worm does not die and the fire is not quenched"* (Mk. 9:43-49).

These, of course, are just images. The reality will be much more frightening. *"Words cannot describe the horror of Hell. We will cry but no-one will show us sympathy. We will moan but no-one will hear us. We will sigh and no-one will pay us any attention. We will look all around us in agony but we will not find comfort from anywhere. Oh! What misery, what wretched plight of the souls which will be found in this condition"* (St. John Chrysostom, *Themata Zoës Vol I.* p. 71 [in Greek]).

All those sufferings will torment man's body, but the soul will also be tormented, which will be much more painful.

a. The first and main torment will be the a b s e n c e o f G o d ' s p r e s e n c e. The soul will be cut off from God forever and will lose every communication with Him. There is nothing more terrible than this. Ultimately, Hell is the absence of God, whereas Paradise is the presence of God.

b. H a v i n g a g u i l t y c o n s c i e n c e is the second torment of the soul. The sins will be presented constantly before the soul and the guilt will torture it, but without any result.

c. The third torment which the soul will suffer is the i n d e - s c r i b a b l e s h a m e which the sinner will feel. All his deeds will be revealed and everyone will see them. St. Basil the Great says that this shame which the soul will experience will be even greater and more frightful than the darkness and the eternal fire.

d. Finally, the sinner will be constantly together with the evil and hideous d e m o n s, who will be proud that they managed to conquer him and drag him into their dark kingdom to suffer eternally together with them.

"Eternal"

Regardless of how terrifying these descriptions are, there is something even more frightful, which destroys all hope. Hell will be for eternity. It will never end, never. There, death will be immortal. If Hell would end in a million years —as the saying goes— regardless of how terrible it would be, it would have an end. But Hell —oh woe!— will have no end! This is the most terrifying of all.

Why eternal?

A question which is often raised is: Why does God, for a few years of sinning, punish a person for all eternity? How can God's l o v e for mankind (His philanthropy) agree with Him being able to watch His creation suffer eternally? How can this be compared to God's j u s t i c e ? Is it right that for few years of sins man should be condemned for all eternity? What answer will we give to this?

A. Firstly, no one can doubt God's l o v e for mankind. Whoever has sinned and truly repented has found the gate of Paradise open. And if every sinner would repent, everyone would enter Paradise, for God *"desires all men to be saved"* (1Ti. 2:4).

Hell was not created for man; it was *"for the devil and his angels"* (Matt. 25:41), because the demons are unrepentant. It is the same for the unrepentant sinners. The soul of the person who willingly persists in sinning, h a r d e n s . This condition is permanent and incurable. Consequently, the unrepentant sinners imitate the demons, who remain indifferent before God's love.

God's love cannot remedy this condition of hardening unless He abolishes man's freedom. But God never violates man's free will. He does not want to save us by force or compulsion.

In the end, man himself chooses Hell when he freely surrenders to sin, which makes his nature like that of the demons.

In this condition, even if God placed him in Paradise, it would been impossible for him to stay there – he wouldn't be able to endure it. Thus St. Paul advises: *"Exhort one another daily, while it is called 'Today,' lest any of you be hardened through the deceitfulness of sin"* (Heb. 3:13).

B. Concerning the second part of the question: why a sinful life of a few years should be punished with eternal Hell and how can it compare with God's R i g h t e o u s n e s s, we answer as follows:

a. Firstly, something similar happens in human terms. A crime, e.g. a murder, is committed in one moment. But the murderer is condemned to a life sentence, or is executed.

b. Sin is temporary, but the God whose laws we violate is infinite and eternal. And he who dares to sin scorns not human laws, but the laws of the eternal and almighty Law-giver.

c. God eternally punishes a temporary sin, because He does not consider the deed as much as the i n t e n t i o n of man. We cannot say that whoever dies unrepentant has stopped sinning. If he lived eternally on earth, he would sin eternally. *"The person who persists in sinning until his last breath and does not repent, will continue to sin eternally, if death did not end his life. That's why he receives eternal punishment by the righteous judgment of God"*(Macarios of Patmos, *Evang. Salpinx* p. 317 [in Greek]).

d. God's righteousness is manifested even in Hell, because in Hell there are various degrees of punishments. Not everyone will be punished to the same degree. This is supported by Christ's words: *"And that servant who knew his master's will, and did not... do according to his will, shall be beaten with many blows. But he who did not know, yet committed things worthy of stripes, shall be beaten with few."* (Lk. 12:47-48). This shows the difference in the degree of punishment (see Matt. 10:15; 11:21-24).

20.2. PARADISE

Indescribable beauty

Let us now examine Paradise. Right from the beginning we must point out that the Paradise we will be talking about is not the Garden of Eden where God first placed Adam and Eve. That Paradise was an earthly one. The Paradise in which the righteous will live after the Second Coming will be heavenly and eternal.

There are no words to describe the beauty and the blessedness of Paradise. St. Paul, who in his life-time was honored to go to Paradise, says that: *"Eye has not seen, nor ear heard, nor has entered into the heart of man the things which God has prepared for those who love Him"* (1Cor. 2:9).

Some of the different categories of the saints in Paradise

Images of Paradise

Holy Scripture, as well as providing images concerning Hell, also provides a few images to give us an idea about Paradise. But these images, like those of Hell, are also very poor descriptions of its reality. The first image is its name, P a r a d i s e, which means a garden with exquisite trees, with running water, singing birds, etc. Paradise is also described as an e l i t e B a n q u e t (Lk. 14:16) prepared by the heavenly Father; it is compared to a royal W e d - d i n g (Matt. 22:2-14), and more.

The most majestic image of Paradise is that which is described in the Book of Revelation of St. John (the *Apocalypse*). It is the Heavenly City which God has prepared as a dwelling-place for His children; a place of eternal joy (see Rev. 21:10). St. John says: *"I saw a new heaven and a new earth ... the holy city, New Jerusalem, coming down out of heaven from God, prepared as a bride adorned for her husband* [Jesus Christ]. *And I heard a loud voice from heaven saying: Behold, the tabernacle of God is with men, and He will dwell with them, and they shall be His people. God Himself will be with them"* (Rev. 21:1-3). So that's what Paradise is – the dwelling of God together with man.

Next, St. John describes Paradise using symbolism. In his vision, this city was built out of pure gold and crystal, and precious stones and pearls. It was completely illuminated with God's glory. But it had no temple. Why? Because the temple was God Himself. Neither a sun nor a moon existed to illuminate it, because the glory of God illuminated it. From the Throne of God flowed the *"River of Life."* In Paradise the new Tree of Life existed.

In this city joy will reign. The Evangelist assures us, that God will *"wipe away every tear from their* [the inhabitants'] *eyes; there shall be no more death, nor sorrow, nor crying. There shall be no more pain, for the former things have passed away"* (Rev. 21:4). Whoever will live here, will gaze upon the face of God with joy and will reign with Him unto the ages of ages.

And who are those blessed who will live eternally there? No sinner or impure person, neither anyone who loves falsehood and evil, but only all those who are faithful to the Lamb, i.e. Christ, and are written in the Book of Life.

There will be no natural or moral evil. Continuous progress

Let us see now what the life of the righteous will be like in the Kingdom of Heaven. Firstly, in Paradise the devil will not exist to scandalize us and lead us into temptation. No evil, neither natural or moral, will exist. *"Here on earth there is the great danger of falling into sin. There, such a danger does not exist. There is no pain or illness... but the land of the living where no-one will die because of sin, but they will live the true life, the life in Christ"* (St. Basil the Great, On Ps. 114/(115); EPE 5, 412-414 [in Greek]).

In Paradise there will be no stagnancy. Man will p r o g r e s s continuously and will ascend to higher and holier spiritual levels. His knowledge and experience of God will grow continuously. Man will ever-increasingly enjoy the divine gifts and the more he receives, the more he will want – he will never feel as if it is enough.

The completion of deification – the vision of God

The highest purpose for which man was created, to become *"in the likeness"* of God, will be eventualized in the kingdom of God – man will become like God. There, the faithful will become *"partakers of the divine nature"* as the apostle Peter mentions (2Pt. 1:4). *"This will be the future life to come,"* says St. Symeon of Thessalonica; *"God will be with us, we shall see Him and communicate with Him"* (About the holy Liturgy, P.G. 155, 258AB [in Greek]).

St. John the Theologian and Evangelist mentions the following significant point: *"When Christ will be revealed* [at His Second Coming,] *we shall be like Him, for we shall see Him as He is"* (1Jn. 3:2). The sight of God will make man *resemble* God. This will be the source of indescribable joy and blessedness which the righteous will feel in Paradise.

In order to comprehend the joy we will feel at seeing God, let us recall the event of Christ's Transfiguration. On Mount Tabor the Lord was transfigured – He shone like the sun. All His body shone with divine glory. This sight caused so much joy to His disciples, that Peter said to Christ: *"Lord, it is good for us to be here. If you wish, let us make here three tents...* [to stay forever here]*"* (Matt. 17:1-4). And what they saw was just a small part of His glory.

The righteous will shine like the sun

The righteous will not only see this glory, but will receive it and reflect it. Christ assured us saying that *"the righteous will shine forth as the sun in the kingdom of their Father"* (Matt. 13:43).

Here we must point out that the more pure and holy one is, the more he will shine and radiate the light of the divine glory. That is, in Paradise there will also be various levels or degrees, just as in Hell (see 1Cor. 15:41).

Knowledge of God

Besides seeing God and besides the illumination that the righteous will receive and radiate, they will experience something even more profound. They will progress continuously in the knowledge of God, in knowing the Holy Trinity. This knowledge is not theoretical and superficial but deep and empirical. Christ in His prayer said that eternal life is to know the True God and Jesus Christ (see Jn. 17:3). But, we need to emphasize once more, that when we speak about the sight of God, the knowledge of God, etc., we do not refer to God's Essence but to His Energies (see chapter 2.2).

The continuously increasing knowledge of God will increase the love of the faithful towards Christ who is the reason for their salvation. Then they will understand the deeper meaning of Christ's work of redemption. Then they will comprehend the Incarnation, they will better understand the mystery of the Sacrifice on the Cross and all the other works of divine Economy.

Communication between the righteous

Besides the communication which the righteous will have with God, they will also communicate amongst themselves. All those who are worthy —and we hope that all of us will be worthy— of the kingdom of God, will live in utmost unity. There will be no coldheartedness or misunderstandings, differences in opinion or selfishness; and not even a shadow of malice, envy, spite or egotism. Perfect understanding, love and brotherhood will reign.

Then, the Lord's desire and request that *"they all may be one"* (Jn. 17:21) will be fulfilled to the utmost degree. The love and unity that reigns between the Persons of the Holy Trinity, will exist between the faithful. The sight of the other souls will increase the joy and happiness of the righteous.

There, each of us will meet with our parents, siblings, children, friends and relatives. We will see once again all those who we loved, young and beautiful. Death will no longer separate us from them.

And if we don't see some of our beloved in Paradise, which means that they are in Hell, won't we feel sorry for them? We do not know how God will provide, in this situation. It is suggested that God will remove them from our memory in order that we not sorrow for their being lost for eternity. Or perhaps the exultation we feel, will overpower and remove the sadness.

Finally, in Paradise we will meet and recognize the saints. We will see our forefathers Adam and Eve, Abraham, Moses and all the righteous of the Old Testament. We will see St. John the Baptist, the Holy Apostles, the Holy Fathers, the martyrs and all the other saints, known and unknown. Above all, we will see the All-Holy Mother of God, our sweet *Panagia,* who helped so much with her intercessions and prayers for the salvation of us sinners.

Present and future life

We attempted to give a faint description of what is Paradise. Our knowledge of the metaphysical world is very small. As much as the difference between the knowledge of an infant is to that of an adult, so much so is the difference between the knowledge which we now have concerning the future life to come, to that which we will have then, with the grace of God (see: 1Cor. 13:9-11).

Paradise is the purpose of our life. God created us to live in Paradise. And to make us heirs of His Kingdom, He did not even spare offering His only-begotten Son, Who He offered as a sacrifice upon the Cross in order to ensure us of His eternal blessings.

Hell is a great evil... We were terrified hearing of the inde-scribable torments which the condemned will suffer; and the worst is, that it is eternal. But as strange as it may seem, a far greater misfortune than to be found in Hell, is to be deprived of Paradise, to be denied of all the blessings which God has pre-pared for us.

So what is this present life? It is like a dream, a shadow, a va-por which vanishes (see Jam. 4:14). Nevertheless, this short and temporary life, which is a drop of water compared to the ocean of eternity, h a s i n f i n i t e v a l u e. Because the acquisition of eternal life depends on how we make good use of the few years which we will live on this earth. It depends on how we will use the short time we have in our hands, before the curtain falls on the stage of our life. As you can understand, we all have a huge responsibility to make good use of our short earthly life; some-thing very small, which, however, has infinite value.

We close with the words of the apostle Paul who addresses the faithful of all the ages, and which summarizes the whole moral and dogmatic teaching of our Church:

"For the grace of God that brings salvation has appeared to all men, teaching us that, denying ungodliness and worldly lusts, we should live soberly, righteously, and godly in the present age, looking for the blessed hope and glorious ap-pearing of our great God and Savior Jesus Christ, who gave Himself for us, that He might redeem us from every lawless deed and purify for Himself His own special people, zealous for good works." (Tts. 2:11-14).

To Him be the glory and the power unto the ages. Amen.

IN SUMMARY

Every Christian must know two basic things very well: **orthodoxy** (correct faith) and **orthopraxia** (correct deeds). Both are equally needful for our salvation.

The Orthodox Christian Faith is founded upon **Holy Scripture** (the written word of God) and **Holy Tradition** (the unwritten word of God).

The primary truth of our faith is that **God exists**. God is immaterial and invisible, He is manifested to man through His works. His existence is testified to by the amazing universe which we see around us.

God is omnipresent, almighty/omnipotent, eternal, omniscient, holy, righteous, love, and more.

The second basic truth is the dogma of the **Holy Trinity:** that God is One in Essence (Nature), but three Persons: **Father, Son and Holy Spirit.** The source of the Deity is the Father, from whom the Son is "begotten" and the Holy Spirit "proceeds." The three Persons are *homoousios* (consubstantial) having one and the same Essence. Each of the three Persons are wholly and entirely God. The Father is perfect God, the Son is perfect God and the Holy Spirit is perfect God. However they are not three Gods, but One.

Out of love, God created the entire Cosmos; the visible (natural) world and the invisible world (the angels). He created it from nothing, using only His word.

The angels were the first creation of God. The **angels** are spirits; rational and immortal. Their work is to glorify God, to serve His Will, and to undertake the work concerning the salvation of mankind.

One of the angels, Lucifer, wanted to become god, thus he fell from Heaven dragging with him a part of the angelic hosts. All these became evil spirits; these are the **demons.**

After the angels, God created the natural world; the stars, the sun, the Earth, the plants, the fish, the birds, the animals. He created everything in six days.

Last of all, God created **man**. Man is a composite hypostasis. He consists of two elements: body (matter) and soul (spirit). He was made in the *"image"* of God, i.e. with divine characteristics such as logic and free-will, with the purpose of reaching the *"likeness,"* of God: to become like God in holiness.

After the creation of the world, God never ceased showing interest for it. This interest and continual concern of God for the world is called **Divine Providence**. Without Divine Providence the universe would have remained ungoverned and would been destroyed.

Once God made **Adam** and **Eve,** (the *protoplastous*) He placed them in a beautiful garden which He had prepared for them - **Paradise**. There they lived in unlimited joy and blessedness.

In Paradise man was to progress towards his final purpose, to be *"in the likeness"* of God. He would have achieved this with God's help, but also by his own efforts. For this reason God gave Adam and Eve one **commandment** which they had to obey. The commandment was not to eat from the tree of the *"knowledge of good and evil."* If they were to eat of it, they would die.

Eventually being deceived by the devil, Adam and Eve disobeyed the commandment and sinned. The result was their exile from Paradise, to live with hardship, tears and pain, until they would be led to the frightful end, death - that is, to return back to the earth from which they were taken. The **ancestral** or **original sin** and its results were transmitted like an inherited illness to the entire human race.

With the passing of time, man stopped believing in the true God and started to worship nature and the lifeless **idols** (statues). At the same time, the **morality** of men degenerated to an unthinkable state. Additionally, **society** became like Hell. Evil, injustice, savagery and crime had reached their limits. Pain, hopelessness, and desperation reigned everywhere.

Nobody could have saved man from this condition. And here God displayed His infinite wisdom and love. God found a way to cure evil. He sent His Son into the world to save us. This work of God for the salvation of man from sin is called **"Divine Economy/ Dispensation"** or **"work of redemption."**

It was for our salvation, therefore, that the only-begotten Son and Word of God, the second Person of the Holy Trinity, took up flesh and **became incarnate;** He received flesh and blood from the All-holy Theotokos and became man, our Lord Jesus Christ. In the person of Christ, the two natures were united, the divine and the human. Christ is perfect God and perfect man. He is the unique **God-Man**. As Man He is similar to us in everything besides sin. As God He is consubstantial with the Father and the Holy Spirit.

In Holy Scripture we see Christ acting as God (performing miracles, forgiving sins, reading the thoughts of men), and in other circumstances acting as a human being (hungering, thirsting, becoming tired, sleeping, suffering, dying).

The work of redemption of Christ occurred in different stages:

With His teaching, Christ freed us from the error of idolatry and revealed the true God to us.

With His crucifixion and death, Christ abolished sin and reconciled man to God.

With His descent into Hades, Christ became victorious over the devil and freed the souls which were held under the devil's authority.

With His Resurrection, Christ conquered death and granted us eternal Life.

Finally, with His Ascension, Christ rose into the Heavens and sat at the right hand of God, raising with Him our human nature, to which He was united.

Ten days after the Ascension, on the day of Pentecost, Christ sent into the world the **Holy Spirit**, the third person of the Holy Trinity, which descended upon the holy apostles and established the Church. Since that day, the Holy Spirit remains within the Church, strengthening and sanctifying it's members. The Holy Spirit consecrates the Holy Mysteries, enlightens the preachers of the Gospel, performs miracles, strengthens the martyrs, manifests the saints, and comforts and enlightens the faithful.

The **Church** is a *Theanthropical* institution (with a divine and human nature). The leader and head of the Church is Christ and its members are all the faithful, who are considered the Body of Christ. The **purpose** of the Church is to utilize Christ's Work of Redemption and to continue it until this world ends. Consequently, the Church's purpose is man's salvation by leading him to God.

The **means** which the Church uses are **preaching** God's word; **Divine Grace**, which is granted through the Holy Sacraments or Mysteries; and **shepherding** the faithful, i.e. the concern for and preservation of the faithful from spiritual dangers.

The Church consists of two parts: the **Church Militant** (the faithful who live on this earth and struggle the spiritual struggle) and the **Church Triumphant** (consisting of those who have passed into the next life). There is communication between these two parts; each of them prays for the other. The Church consists of the **clergy** (deacons, presbyters/priests and bishops) and the **laity**. In the Orthodox Church, the **Oecumenical Synods** are the supreme authority. All the bishops take part in these synods.

The Church is **One**, since Christ, it's Head, is one. It is **Holy,** since it's Head, Christ, is holy. It is **Catholic**, because it has as its mission, to spread throughout the entire world, and because it contains the entire truth. Finally, the Church is **Apostolic,** because it has the holy apostles as it's founders.

This one, holy, catholic and apostolic Church is the Orthodox Church, because only the Orthodox Church safeguarded the Faith which Christ and the apostles passed on to us. The other denominations (Catholic, Protestants etc.) changed their faith and the decisions of the Oecumenical Synods.

The Church sanctifies the faithful through the Grace of the Holy Mysteries or Sacraments. There are seven **Sacraments:** Baptism, Chrismation, Holy Eucharist or Holy Communion, Confession, Marriage, Priesthood and Holy Unction.

The first and most essential Sacrament is **Baptism,** through which one becomes a member of the Church. Through this Sacrament man is granted forgiveness of the Ancestral/Original Sin and all other sins. Baptism is a second birth, a supranatural birth, which initiates man into a new way of life.

The second fundamental Sacrament is **Holy Communion,** in which the faithful partake of the Body and Blood of Christ, which grants eternal life.

After the descent of the Holy Spirit and the institution of the Church, the world will enter into its final stage of history, the **"last days" (eschatology)** which will end with the Second Coming of Christ. According to Christ's clear declaration, the Lord will come again to judge the world.

On that frightful day, four major events will take place: a) the **end of the world**, when all the universe will be destroyed so that a new and imperishable world will appear; b) The **Second Coming**, during which the Lord will come with all His glory, accompanied by all the angels; c) The **Resurrection of the dead**, when all the bodies of the dead will be re-created; the souls which had been separated from the bodies by death will return, and the bodies will come to life; and finally d) **the Universal Judgment**, where Christ will judge all men according to their deeds.

After the Second Coming and the Universal Judgment, will come the **"future age,"** infinite eternity, which will have two states of being: eternal life **(Paradise)** which the righteous will enjoy; and eternal **Hell,** where the unrepentant sinners will suffer for all eternity.

ENGLISH BIBLIOGRAPHY

1. THE ORTHODOX STUDY BIBLE, NEW KING JAMES VERSION Thomas Nelson Inc, 2008.

2. THE HOLY BIBLE, NEW KING JAMES VERSION Thomas Nelson Publishers, 1987.

3. OXFORD THESAURUS OF ENGLISH.

4. ORTHODOX DOGMATIC THEOLOGY Fr. Michael Pomazansky, translated by Hieromonk Seraphim Rose, St. Herman of Alaska Brotherhood.

5. THE MYSTERY OF DEATH Nikolaos P. Vassiliadis, translated by Fr. Peter A. Chamberas, The Orthodox Brotherhood of Theologians "The Savior" 1993.

6. OUR ORTHODOX CHRISTIAN FAITH Athanasios S. Frangopoulos The Orthodox Brotherhood of Theologians "The Savior" 1984.

7. OXFORD GREEK-ENGLISH LEARNER'S DICTIONARY D.N. Stavropoulos, Oxford University Press 2012.

8. SACRED CATECHISM OF THE ORTHODOX CHURCH Demetrios N. Vernardakis, translated by Claude Delaval Cobham, Institute for Byzantine and Modern Greek Studies 2004.

9. GENESIS CREATION AND EARLY MAN, THE ORTHODOX CHRISTIAN VISION Fr. Seraphim Rose, St. Herman of Alaska Brotherhood, 2011.

10. MY EXODUS FROM ROMAN CATHOLICISM His Grace Bishop Paul de Ballester, St. Nicodemus Publications, 2011.

11. FEASTS OF THE LORD Metropolitan Nafpaktos Hierotheos, Birth of the Theotokos Monastery, 2nd Edition 2013.

BIBLIOGRAPHY IN GREEK

1. Αγ. Κυρίλλου Ιεροσολύμων, *Κατηχήσεις*, Εκδ. «Ετοιμασία», Ι. Μονή Τιμίου Προδρόμου Καρέας, 1999.
2. Αγ. Ιωάννου Δαμασκηνού, *Έκδοσις ακριβής Ορθοδόξου Πίστεως*, Εκδ. Πουρνάρα, Θεσσ., 1985.
3. Αγ. Συμεών Θεσσαλονίκης, *Το Σύμβολον της Πίστεως*, μετάφραση Γ. Μαυρομάτη, Έκδ. «Επέκτασις», 1997.
4. Αγ. Νικοδήμου Αγιορείτου, *Εορτοδρόμιον*, Έκδ. «Ορθόδοξος Κυψέλη», Θεσ/νίκη, 1987. *Νέα Κλίμαξ*, Έκδ. Β. Ρηγοπούλου, Θεσ/νίκη, 1976.
5. Μητροπ. Ναυπάκτου Ιεροθέου, *Οι Δεσποτικές εορτές*, Ι. Μονή Γενεθλίου Θεοτόκου (Πελαγίας), 1998.
6. Μητροπ. Αντινόης Παντελεήμονος, *Η Ορθόδοξη Χριστιανική Διδασκαλία*, Γιαννιτσά, 2009.
7. Μητροπ. Κονίτσης Σεβαστιανού, *«Πιστεύω ...»*, Έκδ. Αδελφ. Θεολ. «Ο Σωτήρ», Αθήνα, 1999.
8. Πρωτοπρ. Κωνσταντίνου Καλλινίκου, *Τα θεμέλια της Πίστεως*, Έκδ. Πουρνάρα, Θεσ/νίκη, 1976.
9. Πρωτοπρ. Αντωνίου Αλεβιζοπούλου, *Η Ορθοδοξία μας*, Αθήνα, 1994.
10. Αρχιμ. Αστερίου Χατζηνικολάου, *Μέλλουσα Κρίση και Αιωνιότητα*, Έκδ. Αδελ. Θεολ. «Ο Σωτήρ», Αθήνα, 2009.
11. Πρωτοπρ. Στεφάνου Κ. Αναγνωστοπούλου, *Γνώση και βίωμα της Ορθοδόξου Πίστεως*, Πειραιάς, 2006.
12. Μοναχού Νικοδήμου Μπιλάλη, *Ορθόδοξη Πίστη και Λατρεία*, Οργανισμός Εκδόσεως Διδακτικών Βιβλίων, Αθήνα, 1977.
13. *Πιστεύω εις ένα Θεόν*, Θέματα φιλικών κύκλων, Έκδ. Αδελφ. Θεολ. «Ζωή», Αθήνα 1996.
14. Κων. Μπόνη, *Κατήχησις και Λειτουργική*, Επικοιν. και Μορφωτ. Υπηρεσία της Εκκλησίας της Ελλάδος, Αθήνα, 2005.
15. Αθανασίου Φραγκοπούλου, *Η Ορθόδοξος Χριστιανική Πίστις μας*, Έκδ. Αδελφ. Θεολ. «Ο Σωτήρ», Αθήνα, 1999.
16. Ανδρέα Θεοδώρου, *Η ουσία της Ορθοδοξίας*, Έκδ. «Περιστερά», Αθήνα, 1961.
17. Ανδρέα Θεοδώρου, *Πιστεύω εις ένα Θεόν*, Έκδ. Αποστολικής Διακονίας, 2007.
18. Νικολάου Σωτηροπούλου, *Αντιχιλιαστικόν εγχειρίδιον*, Έκδ. Ορθοδ. Ιεραπ. Αδελφ. «Ο Σταυρός», Αθήνα, 1994.
19. Νικολάου Βασιλειάδη, *Το μυστήριον του θανάτου*, Έκδ. Αδελφ. Θεολ. «Ο Σωτήρ», Αθήνα, 1991.